CHICHI BIS[...]

TEACH US TO *Pray*

Tudor Bismark Ministries
P. O. Box 58966, London, SE6 9HB.
www.TudorBismark.org.uk

All rights reserved. No part of this publication may be reproduced, stored in a retrieval system, or transmitted in any form or by any means—for example, electronic, photocopy, and recording—without the prior written permission of the publisher. The only exception is brief quotations in printed reviews.

All scripture quotations are from the KJV, MKJV, NKJV and ISV versions of the Bible.

Book Services By:

Moore Creative Services
www.moorecreative.org
Contact: Lisa Moore, lisa@ moorecreative.org

©2012 by Tudor Bismark Ministries
All rights reserved.

FORWARD

Leading a ministry has numerous and many times unreasonable challenges. Many of these challenges are spiritually related and must therefore be addressed by intense intercessory prayer. From the onset of our marriage and ministry experience, Chi Chi, affectionately called "Ma" by our church members, began a regimented prayer discipline, prayer culture, and prayer style in the early 1980's. Of all the intercessors I have had interaction with in different parts of the world, Chi Chi is in the top five (Gwen Shaw, Cindy Jacobs, Lila Terhune, Florence Cook, Chi Chi Bismark). Her passion and anointing for prayer is truly remarkable; along with her boldness and tenacity to obtain results. Many around the world can testify and have witnessed firsthand, the significance of her gift.

I have watched Chi Chi grow in prayer, and witnessed God's grace increase on her life significantly, not only in prayer, but also as a prophetic teacher and preacher. This book is the first of many that will be produced from her revelation, and her prayer journey that comprises a plethora of experiences from a range of people, groups, ministries and countries.

I truly believe that this book will impact your life, and that the numerous principles will produce lasting and meaningful results for you, your family, your ministries and your nation.

Tudor Bismark (Greatest Fan)

TEACH US TO PRAY

DEDICATION

I dedicate this book to my God who has taught me all I know about prayer. My zeal and passion for prayer comes from the Holy Spirit and my heart is full with the knowledge of where the journey has taken me.

To my four boys who have kept me on my knees in prayer from the day they were born. I have also experienced the joy of teaching each of them how to pray from a very young age. I have watched them be committed and faithful to prayer and this has been a tremendous blessing.

To my husband who has been by my side in spiritual warfare. May the Lord richly bless you and impart to you a greater measure of revelation.

TEACH US TO PRAY

CONTENTS

PART ONE—Types of Prayer	11
Different Strokes for Different Types	13
Thanksgiving Prayer	15
Praise & Worship Prayer	19
Intercession	22
Travail	26
Groaning	29
Supplication and Petition	32
Blessing Prayer	36
Confession of Sins	38
Confession of the Word	40
Declaration Prayer	42
Decrees	45
Directed Prevailing Prayer	48
Shouting & Yelling Prayer	50
Metaphoric Prayer	53
Demonstration & Dedication Prayer	55
Sacks and Ashes Prayer	57
Praying in the Spirit	59
Concert Prayer	61
Spiritual Warfare Prayer	63
Meditation Prayer	66
Weeping Prayer	68
Apostolic Rank Prayer	70
Prophetic Prayer	72
Sacrificial Prayer	74
PART TWO—Why Pray?	77
Additional notes on why you should pray	80

PART THREE—The Heavenly Court System	85
The Divine Council	86
PART FOUR—Effectual Fervent Prayer	93
Prayers of Repentance	93
Thanksgiving	96
Proclamations, Decrees and Declarations	102
Declare, Decree, Proclaim	109
Jubilee and Favor	110
Intercession	112
Apostolic Decrees of Justice and Peace	113
Prayer and Declaration for the Leaders of the City	114
The Lord's Prayer	116
Prayers from Psalm 91	117
INDEX	119

TEACH US TO PRAY

PART I
TYPES OF PRAYER

There are a variety of prayers and it is important as believers, to possess the full arsenal of prayer with which God has equipped us. An effective soldier in any army has the ability to effectively deal with the enemy and enforce victory even in difficult circumstances. The United States Military has over 498 known different types of conventional offensive weaponry.[1] Over the years they have developed a variety of weapon systems to cater for and combat different enemies in different situations.

Christians must know that every battle or situation we face requires a specific type of prayer engagement in order to enforce the victory that is ours.

We too as believers have been engaged in the oldest war known to man, since the fall of Lucifer. We need to know that we are in a fight, and our enemies are not carnal but spiritual.[2] God has given us many spiritual weapons in prayer that we can use. He says in Ephesians 6:18 *"...praying always with ALL manner of prayer..."* Just like the military has different weapons for different situations, we Christians must know that every battle or situation we face requires a specific type of prayer engagement in order to enforce the victory that is ours.

My husband and I pastor a church in the city of Harare, Zimbabwe. If you know anything about the history of Zimbabwe, you will know of the struggles and turmoil this nation has suffered. You will know of war, of drought and of economic meltdown. You will know of systematic poverty and food shortages. If you know anything about building a church, you will know the pain of growing a church, the despair of not having enough resources, the disappointment of losing good people and the frustration of running a large organization. But today, we stand strong as a church and as a people. Our church is growing and thriving. Our people are beginning to influence the marketplace and government leaders and impact communities for the Kingdom of God. We are taking back what was stolen by the enemy; we are taking back our marriages; we are taking back our children; we are taking back our finances. We know that every victory we have today was birthed in prayer—not just one type, but all manner of prayer. Our God is God of strategy; He has given us strategies on how to pray over different situations.

The Bible says, *"...He guides us in ALL things..."* In our walk with Him over the years, God has revealed to us wondrous truth from His Word about prayer. I want to share this truth with you. My prayer for you is that this book should cause you to "raise the standard" in your walk with Him—for you to be like Elijah—who prayed the rain to stop and it stopped; who prayed the rain to come and it rained; and who prayed fire to fall from heaven and fire fell down.

The Holy Spirit has revealed to me twenty-four powerful types of prayer; together we will explore these truths and after reading this book, you will realize that the devil will have no place to hide from you.

PART ONE — TYPES OF PRAYER

Different Strokes for Different Types

Consider for a moment. Would you take your 1.6 liter sedan to visit your grandmother in the rural mountainous outback or would you take your 3.0 liter 4WD SUV? Would you go swimming in your swimsuit or in a Giorgio Armani suit? Is there any logic in taking a knife to a gunfight? These appear to be simple examples, but for many Christians engaging in spiritual battles, this logic does not appear to be as obvious.

Too often in the spirit realm we go into gunfights with a knife. We go to the devil swinging our knives while the devil stands cocked and loaded with a double barrel shotgun. The outcome is inevitable. The Bible says, *"My people perish for a lack of knowledge."* [1] Isaiah 5:13 also says *"...My people go into captivity because they have no knowledge..."* Many Christians today have lost their faith. They are left in debt, are stuck in sickness and are left frustrated wondering why their prayers remain unanswered.

The twelve disciples were right in asking, *"Lord, teach us to pray."* [2] My heart's cry for the Body of Christ is that we would get wisdom and revelation of how we ought to pray. Malachi 2:17 states, *"You have wearied the Lord with your words..."* It is important for us to know how to pray as we endeavor to live powerful, effective, and fulfilled lives in Christ.

In Exodus 14:10–18, the Israelites were caught up between the Red Sea and Pharaoh's army:

And when Pharaoh drew near, the children of Israel lifted their eyes, and behold, the Egyptians marched after them. So they were afraid, and the children of Israel cried out to the Lord. Then they said to Moses, 'Because there were no graves in Egypt, have you taken us away to die in the wilderness? Why have you so dealt with us, to bring us out of Egypt? Is this not the word that we told you in Egypt, saying, 'Let us alone that we may serve the Egyptians. For it would be better to serve the Egyptians than die in the wilderness' And Moses said to the people, Do not be afraid. Stand still, and see the salvation of the Lord, which He will accompany for you today. For the Egyptians you see today, you shall see no more forever. The Lord will fight for you and you shall hold your peace.' And the Lord said to Moses, 'Why do you cry to Me? Tell the children of Israel to go forward. But lift up your rod, and stretch out your hand over the sea and divide it. And the children of Israel will go on dry ground through the midst of the sea.'

Now, why does the Lord say, *"Why do you cry to Me?"* Can He not see that His children were facing certain death? Could He not see the steely murderous looks on the Egyptians faces? Could He not see the shiny glistening metal from the Egyptians' sword ready to spill blood? Of course He could see all this but He still says, *"Why do you cry to Me?"* I believe that God was trying to show Moses and the Israelites that the spiritual atmosphere did not require them to make petitions and requests but for them to make declarations and command the situation into their favor. We can clearly see that Moses had the faith and believed that God would save them but He did not know how to pray through the situation until God showed him.

How many times have we made petition when the situation required thanksgiving? How many times have we made quick short prayers of petition when the situation required that we travail? How many times have you prayed over a situation alone when you should have stood in a prayer of agreement with another believer? This is why we should ask the Lord, "Teach us how to pray." The effectual fervent prayer of a righteous man avails much.³ Our prayers need to be effective.

 *We can no longer afford to be powerless in this perverse generation.*

My brother and sisters, I encourage you—we can no longer afford to be powerless in this perverse generation. Our prayers must reverberate in the four corners of this earth. God has hidden these things FOR us and not FROM us, and it is to the glory of kings and queens to search them out.⁴

Thanksgiving Prayer

My husband is a soccer fan and has been an avid follower of English football for years now. I am amazed at how loyal and faithful he is to his team whether they are winning or losing. In victory or in defeat, his commitment to the cause is unwavering.

In our Christian walk, this unwavering steadfastness is an important component of our prayer life—especially in our thanksgiving. Paul commands the early church saying *"Rejoice in the Lord always, pray without ceasing, in everything give thanks; for this is the will of God in Christ Jesus for you."* [2] Now Paul instructed the early church to "give thanks in everything"—not only when things are going well! Far too many believers will give thanks only when they get a promotion, when they win that big contract or when something really good happens to them. Do you give thanks when your car breaks down en route to an important meeting; when your husband comes in drunk; or even when there is a death in your family? Surely God has exceptions for such extreme cases? There is nothing to be thankful about in situations like these.

 *During the bad and difficult times, we should give thanks the most.*

On the contrary my brothers and sisters—during the bad and difficult times, we should give thanks the most. When we give thanks in difficult situations, we remember that our God is a good God. We remember His benefits; what He has done for us in the past and we remember that His desire for us is to prosper us. He says, *"... I have*

come to give you life and life more abundantly..." ³ Psalms 138:8 reassures of His promises, *"The Lord will perfect everything that concerns me..."* In the midst of our troubles, it is very difficult to see the goodness of the Lord, but it is in giving thanks that we remember His true desire for us. Thanksgiving activates our faith and gives us the courage to overcome our enemies.

So when your car breaks down on the way to an important meeting, you should pray like this, *"Lord, I might be missing this meeting but I thank You that You said kings and queens will come to me to meet me, to seek the wisdom given to me."* When your husband walks in drunk at 2a.m., you pray, *"Lord, I thank You my husband is a man of God, I thank You he loves his home as Christ loved the church."* When you learn of a death in the family you cry, *"Lord, I thank You that you are the Comforter and the Healer. I thank You that you mend our broken hearts and You comfort our souls in this difficult time."* What powerful prayers. When you pray like this, you laugh in the Devil's face. Sarah said in Genesis 21:6, *"God made me laugh, and all who hear will laugh with me."* When in difficult circumstances, the devil will expect you to respond in fear but when you respond in thanksgiving, he is resisted and he will flee from you.⁴

We should get into the habit of thanking God throughout the day for the things that happen to us and to others. This prayer is so powerful and dynamic, when it is mixed with other types of prayer; it provokes the heavens to respond to your situation. See Philippians 4:6 which states, *"Be anxious for nothing, but in everything by prayer and supplication, with thanksgiving, let your requests be known to God; and the peace of God which surpasses all understanding will guard your heart and minds through Christ Jesus."*

The effect of un-thankfulness is just as potent as the effect of a thankful attitude. Paul clearly warns us in Romans, saying:

> *...because although they knew God, they did not glorify Him as God, nor were thankful, but became futile in their thoughts, and their foolish hearts were darkened. Professing to be wise, they became fools....therefore God gave them up to uncleanness, in the lusts of their hearts... who exchange the truth of God for a lie...For this reason God gave them to vile passions. For even their women exchanged the natural use for what is against nature. Likewise also the men, leaving the natural use of the woman, burned in their lusts for one another...being filled with all unrighteousness, sexual immorality, wickedness, covetousness, maliciousness, full of envy, murder, strife, deceit, evil-mindedness; they are whisperers, back-biters, haters of God, violent, proud, boasters, undiscerning, untrustworthy, unloving, unforgiving, unmerciful...* [5]

 *The effect of un-thankfulness is just as potent as the effect of a thankful attitude.*

WOW! If the effect of un-thankfulness is so potent can you imagine the opposite effect of a thankful spirit? My fellow believers I encourage you to give thanks in every circumstance you find yourself. Do not be like the other nine lepers who forgot to come back and thank the Lord.[6] Sometimes, to see your breakthrough, all you need to do is give thanks.

PART ONE — TYPES OF PRAYER

Praise & Worship Singing

Back to my soccer-loving husband: sometimes I have actually endured watching a match with him. I have watched when a team scores a goal, the way in which the whole stadium erupts into euphoria—the noise, the shouting, the jumping, the clapping, the dancing, the ecstasy. I can imagine that some of the people in the stadium are generally quiet and reserved people, but in this moment, they are beside themselves—embracing strangers, screaming at the top of their lungs and jumping up and down.

When we take the actions of the people in the stadium and direct it towards God; it is called praise and worship. It is an outward and expressive communication to God. It is declaring good things about God, both about His character (who He is) and also about His actions. To say "God is good" is to praise God. Here you are not asking for anything, you are just telling God that you love Him and thank Him for all He has done. The Psalmist says it this way, *"Great is the Lord, and greatly to be praised..."* [1]

Now, there are many styles of praise and worship. In fact, the word praise has over seven different meanings in its original Hebrew language.[2] We will not go into the details of praise and worship—many books have already being written on this subject. However, it is imperative that we know and understand that we were created to praise.[3] The Bible says in Psalms 8:2, *"Out of the mouths of babes and nursing infants, You have ordained praise..."* Now, why does God want our praise so much? Is it because He has a big ego and wants to hear nice things about Himself all the time? Is it because He grows bigger every time He is praised? No, God is BIG already. In fact, He is so BIG, we cannot comprehend His greatness. He holds the universe in the span of His hand. Take that for size. God does not have a big ego, neither does He grow with our praises, but on the contrary, our perception of Him grows in our minds and hearts every time we praise and worship Him. God gets bigger and bigger every time we do this. We begin to believe that nothing is impossible for Him.

 *Our perception of Him grows in our minds and hearts every time we praise and worship Him.*

The reason many believers have a small image of God is because they don't praise and worship Him enough. Hence, they struggle to believe Him for great things. The disciples were amazed that even the sea and the wind obey Him.[4] The Pharisees and the Sadducees were amazed that the demons obeyed and feared Him. Some of you struggle to believe that God heals the sick. Some of you struggle to believe that God can get you out of debt. Some of you struggle to believe that God raises the dead. You struggle to believe these things because your perception of Him is small and you think His abilities are limited. He in Himself is not limited; we are the ones that limit Him. When we praise and worship we begin to receive revelation of how big He is. Worship always precedes revelation. This revelation is the *"enlightened word or rhema word"* that stirs our spirits to accomplish God-inspired feats.

Another question people might ask is this: is praise and worship really a type of prayer? To help answer this, imagine a woman walking in a crowded walkway. She sees her ex-best friend she hasn't seen in ten years. She lets out a scream and runs towards the ex-best friend. The ex-best friend also sees her and she too screams and runs towards her old friend. The two run to each other and embrace in squeals of laughter and excitement. Now, were there any verbal words exchanged? No, not a single word. If you had to translate the shrieks and screams, they would read something like this, "Oh my goodness! Is that you? It is you! You look so beautiful! You are so tall! Your hair...." I am sure most of you can relate to what I am saying with this example. Praise and worship is similar—sometimes there are things we want to express to God that are inexpressible in words, so we express them with shouts and outward manifestations of the body. David is a good example of an individual who prayed to God through praise and worship. Psalm 47:5–7 provides clear instructions on how to praise and worship the Lord: *"God is gone up with a shout, the LORD with the sound of a trumpet. Sing praises to God, sing praises: sing praises unto our King, sing praises. For God is the King of all the earth: sing ye praises with understanding."*

Always take time out during your day to praise and worship Him. Play worship music in the car on your way to work. Sing and hum a psalm while cooking dinner for your family. Lift your hands to Him as you read this book, because the God you serve is a big God and there is nothing that is too hard for Him.

Intercession

Has there been a time in your life where you have had unexpected favor in your business? Or has there being a time where you walked out of a major accident without a scratch? Or maybe a court case swung unexplainably into your favor? Whatever the situation, could these be random cases of luck or good fortune? I do not believe in coincidence and random selection, but I believe that if you have had an unexpected good thing happen to you—maybe someone, somewhere in the world was praying for you. Someone has been making declarations and decrees over your situation. This is the power of intercession prayer.

 *Intercession is love on its knees in prayer for others.*

Intercession is love on its knees in prayer for others. This entails pleading on behalf of the needs of someone else. It is standing in the gap for others. When making intercession, it may entail repenting for other people's sins, or asking God to intervene in someone else's *"life or death"* situation. Whatever the case, intercession prayer is an act of love. It will be impossible to pray for others if you do not love people. The Bible instructs, "For this is the message we heard from the beginning, that we should love one another" [1] And again, *"By this we know love, because He laid down His life for us. And we also ought to lay down our lives for the brethren"* [2] Because God so loved us, He gave up His life to save us; we too should be armed with the same thinking—to lay down our lives for our brothers and sisters because we love them. And the least you can do for others is to pray for them.

The Bible also commands us to love those who even hate us. That is what makes us different from the world. We are able to pray and bless those who persecute us. Many times, I have been prompted by the Holy Spirit to pray for people I do not know and for situations with which I am unfamiliar. Once the burden is lifted off and I sense His peace, I know that whoever or whatever I was praying for will experience a God-ordained intervention. Do not ever ignore the urge or prompting to pray for someone, even if you do not know the person or situation—you could be saving someone's life.

Paul knew the power of the intercession when he said to the Colossian church, *"...praying always for you..."* [3] To the Philippians, *"...always in every prayer of mine making request for you..."* [4] To the Ephesians, *"I do not cease to give thanks for you, making mention of you in my prayers that God..."* [5] And also to the Thessalonians, *"Therefore we also pray always for you that..."* [6] Maybe the reason our churches and businesses are not growing and succeeding is because we are not praying for our members or our employees. When was the last time you prayed for people in your lives—your mail carrier, yardman, or neighbor? Even more alarming—when was the last time you prayed for the teachers who teach your children?

Intercession is not just about interceding for individuals—we can pray for cities and nations too. A good biblical example is Nehemiah, a godly man. He identified with the sins of his people and prayed prayers of repentance, asking the Lord to forgive, to have mercy and to raise up the nation of Israel once again. Nehemiah 1:3–10 says:

> *They said to me, 'Those who survived the exile and are back in the province are in great trouble and disgrace. The wall of Jerusalem is broken down, and its gates have been burned with fire.' When I heard these things, I sat*

down and wept. For some days I mourned and fasted and prayed before the God of heaven. Then I said: '0 LORD, God of heaven, the great and awesome God, who keeps his covenant of love with those who love him and obey his commands let your ear be attentive and your eyes open to hear the prayer your servant is praying before you day and night for your servants, the people of Israel. I confess the sins we Israelites, including myself and my father's house, have committed against you. We have acted very wickedly toward you. We have not obeyed the commands, decrees and laws you gave your servant Moses.'

Daniel is also another good example of an intercessor. In Daniel 9:2–4, he too interceded for the nation of Israel praying:

In the first year of his reign I Daniel understood by books the number of the years, whereof the word of the LORD came to Jeremiah the prophet, that he would accomplish seventy years in the desolations of Jerusalem. And I set my face unto the Lord God, to seek by prayer and supplications, with fasting, and sackcloth, and ashes: And I prayed unto the LORD my God, and made my confession.

Both Daniel and Nehemiah directed the course of their nation by prayer. You do not need to be the President or Mayor to direct the course of your nation—you can do so on your knees in intercession to God. We have seen this happening in countries like Chile and Argentina, where crime, corruption, prostitution and drug use were rampant, but when the saints of God started interceding, all these vices started falling away. Whole neighborhoods were turned to God. Brothels became churches. Government officials returned bribes. It took months and years of prayer—but today Argentina's and Chile's societies are completely transformed from the state they were in twenty years ago.

If your streets are controlled by pimps and thugs—pray. If your schools are infiltrated by drugs and sex—pray. If your government is drowning in corruption—pray. If your home is fueled by alcohol—pray. If your church is perverted by lust and debauchery—pray. God has given us the mandate and our prayers will reach His ears and He will surely intervene and fight for us.

Travail

God often places deep seated burdens in our spirits for which we must travail in prayer until they have been lifted. Many Christians describe this "burden" as a troubling or restlessness of their spirit. In the book of Daniel, King Nebuchadnezzar had dreams; and his spirit was so troubled that his sleep left him.[1] The Bible also says that King Darius, *"went to his palace and spent the night fasting; and no musicians were brought before him. Also his sleep went from him."* [2] King Darius was distressed and sorrowful. Matthew 26:37–38 says, *"And He took with Him Peter and the two sons of Zebedee, and He began to be sorowful and deeply distressed. Then He said to them, 'My soul is exceedingly sorrowful, even to death! Stay here and watch with me.'"* We can see that as the time that the Messiah was to be crucified drew near, He felt the burden of what was ahead and asked Peter, James and John to travail in prayer with him.

Travailing prayers are deep, agonizing *birthing prayers*. They are for pushing issues in the Spirit. Usually the issues that need pushing are of immense importance in your life, in the church or in the nation. You can see that when Jesus went into travail, it was just before the crucifixion—an event that brought salvation to all mankind. When God brings you to the point of travail—be assured; something big is about to shift in your life.

 *When God brings you to the point of travail—be assured; something big is about to shift in your life.*

In child-bearing, the pain and agony form part of the labor process.

The intensity of the contractions increase as the baby prepares to be pushed out of the womb and into the world. Without the pain the expecting mother would risk losing her baby as she would not know when to push—she would not know when to travail. When Jesus was in travail, Luke 22:44, described Him as *"being in agony... And His sweat was as it were great drops of blood falling down to the ground."* The process of travail is one of agony and anguish. But as in the labor room, the travail process has great reward—the joy of hearing your newborn baby coming into this world. Travailing prayers have great reward for one who prays through the agony.

The unique aspect of travailing prayers is that *"we give birth"* to our answers. As human beings, all of us were born and were newborn babies at some stage. Somebody gave birth to us. As believers, we are born again—Christ gave birth to us and made us new creatures.[3] Like Christ, we too as believers give birth to new things. A new thing is a new thing. It did not exist yesterday but it exists today. Isaiah wrote;

> *Behold, the former things have come to pass, and new things I declare; before they happen, I cause you to hear."* [4]
> And again, *"I have foretold the former things from the beginning; and they went out of My mouth; and I made them hear; I acted suddenly; and they came about....And I declared it to you from the beginning. Before it happened I revealed it to you; lest you should say, my idol has done them, and my graven image, and my molten image, has commanded them. You heard; see it all; and will you not declare? I have shown you new things from this time, even hidden things, and you did not know them....They are created now, and not from the beginning; even before the day when you did not hear them; lest you should say, Behold, I knew them.* [5]

When in travail, we give birth to new things. So this means, as a business person, you will give birth to new clients or new streams of income. As a pastor of a church, you will give birth to new congregants in your church. As a medical doctor, you will give birth to new techniques of treating patients.

A scriptural example of this type of prayer is found in Galatians; *"My children, for whom I again travail until Christ should be formed in you..."* [6] Paul here was saying he was determined to continue in travail until he could see the evidence of Christlikeness in his church members. He would remain in the "labor room" until his church was formed or fashioned to resemble Christ. Some people avoid this type of prayer because it is very intense and the agony at times can be overwhelming. We should not avoid this type of prayer but rather when we sense a burden in our spirits, we should be more sensitive to the Holy Spirit. We should persevere and pray through the agony until the burden is lifted.

Isaiah asks the question, *"Shall the earth be made to bring forth in one day? Or shall a nation be born at once?"* Our answer should be, *"...for as soon as Zion travailed, she brought forth her children."* So yes, a nation can be born at once, through our prayers. Our God will not bring us to the point of travail and cause us not to give birth, but rather we will rejoice at the fullness of His glory.

PART ONE — TYPES OF PRAYER

Groaning

Jesus loved a man called Lazarus of Bethany. He was also close to Lazarus's two sisters, Mary and Martha. Jesus loved this family deeply and clearly this family loved and served the Lord too. As we know from Scripture,[1] Lazarus unexpectedly passed away after a short illness. A *"multitude"* [2] of people came to his funeral indicating that Lazarus was a man who impacted and influenced his community for good. Jesus too arrived at the funeral and after meeting Martha and seeing Mary and the Jews weeping, the Bible says, *"...He groaned in the spirit and was troubled..."* [3] Jesus then went to the tomb, and at the tomb, *"Jesus again groaning in Himself,"* [4] instructed for the stone to be rolled away and commanded Lazarus to *"Come out."* [5] We all know what happened—Lazarus arose from the dead.

What is this groaning that Jesus went through? And how come this speechless type of prayer had such power to raise a dead man to life? King David says this, *"Because of the voice of my groaning..."* [6] Clearly, we can see that groaning is an idiom—a form of communication. When we are groaning, our spirits are in communication with the Spirit of God. To fully understand the mystery and power of this type of praying we must know two things. Firstly, that as believers, we are spirit, body and soul. Our spirit is what will live forever because God is Spirit. Our bodies are decaying and will perish forever.

Secondly, from 1 Cor. 2:6–12, we learn that there is a stream of communication between our spirit and the Spirit of God through the Holy Spirit, which we cannot understand intellectually with our minds.

But, we speak wisdom among those who are perfect; yet not the wisdom of this world, nor of the rulers of this world, that come to nothing. But we speak the wisdom of God in a mystery, which God has hidden, predetermining it before the world for our glory; which none of the rulers of this world knew (for if they had known, they would not have crucified the Lord of glory). But as it is written, "Eye has not seen, nor ear heard, nor has it entered into the heart of man, the things which God has prepared for those who love Him. But God has revealed them to us by His Spirit; for the Spirit searches all things, yea, the deep things of God. For who among men knows the things of a man except the spirit of man within him? So also no one knows the things of God except the Spirit of God. But we have not received the spirit of the world, but the Spirit from God, so that we might know the things that are freely given to us by God.

Our spirit speaks the wisdom of God in a mystery. This is similar to many military armies across the world that use encrypted messages to communicate. Their enemies cannot read or understand the messages unless they successfully decode the messages. The Devil cannot decode our groanings; he is powerless to disrupt and frustrate the workings of God.

Even non-believers groan to the Father. The Bibles shows us, saying:

For the earnest expectation of the creation waits for the manifestation of the sons of God. For the creation was not willingly subjected to vanity, but because of Him who subjected it on hope that the creation itself also shall be

> *delivered from the bondage of corruption into the glorious liberty of the children of God. And we know that the whole creation groans and travails in pain together until now. And not only so, but ourselves also, who have the first fruit of the Spirit, even we ourselves groan within ourselves, awaiting adoption, the redemption of our body.* [7]

It is not just we believers that are groaning and crying out to God, but the whole of creation is waiting to be adopted as sons of God. Atheists and non- believers will not admit this or be mentally aware of this but deep down inside, their hearts are calling out to a *"higher being"* to redeem their souls. This is why it is possible for a hardened, murdering criminal to become a son of God because deep down his spirit desires and yearns for something much bigger than himself. King David was right when he said, *"Deep calls onto deep."* [8] Through the groanings of Christ, Lazarus was raised from the dead and through the groanings of creation the whole of creation will have life in Christ.

In groaning prayer we are relying totally on the Holy Spirit to use our faculties, our mind, our body, our voice, and our heart to pray through the purposes of God for an individual or circumstance and or situation. Sometimes the intensity of the will of God is such that it can only manifest through groanings. Romans 8:26–28 says:

> *Likewise the Spirit also helps our infirmities: for we know not what we should pray for as we ought: but the Spirit itself makes intercession for us with groanings which cannot be uttered. And He that searches the hearts knows what is the mind of the Spirit, because He makes intercession for the saints according to the will of God.*

Supplication and Petition

Almost every one of us has prayed a prayer of supplication and petition. Supplication means to petition or entreat someone for something; to make a humble entreaty; especially to pray to God; to ask humbly and earnestly of. As human beings, all of us have needs. Only God is complete in Himself. We need God to make us complete in all things—spiritually, emotionally and physically. That is why He says, *"ask and it shall be given."* [1]

I have not met a person who doesn't have a need. We are all in need. We need money; we need jobs, love, respect, clothes, family, security, health, justice. The list is endless. God earnestly desires for us to ask from Him. It honors Him when we entreat and make petitions to Him. When we ask from Him, we are acknowledging that He is our Source and that He is able and greater than us. A king would not ask and plead money from a beggar. King Solomon said it in this way, *"The poor speaks humble requests, but the rich answers roughly."* [2] The greater always blesses the lesser.[3] In our relationship with God, we are the poorer; God is the greater; so we must not refrain in making supplication and petitions to Him.

I have not met a person who doesn't have a need. We are all in need.

The Bible tells of a king who refused to ask and make supplications to God for help even on his death bed. King Asa became king at a young age. As many of you when you first come into the church, King Asa was full of zeal and energy for the Lord. He even commanded

PART ONE — TYPES OF PRAYER

his nation *"seek Jehovah, the God of their fathers, and to do the Law and the commandment."* [4] God blessed King Asa and the nation of Judah during this time, and King Asa and the people of Judah rebuilt their nation and prospered. King Asa had an army of 580,000 men with shields and spears and *"the land had rest."* [5] However, King Asa's nation was invaded by the Ethiopians, who had n army of 1,000,000 plus 300,000 chariots. King Asa was not only out-gunned, but he was out-numbered too. If you were a gambling man, your bet was safe with the Ethiopians. However:

> *King Asa cried to Jehovah his God and said, 'Jehovah, it is nothing with You to help, whether with many or with him who has no power. Help us, 0 Jehovah our God, for we rest on You, and in Your name we go against this multitude. 0 Jehovah, You are our God. Do not let man prevail against You.'* [6]

King Asa made supplication to God, for Him to save and deliver Judah from the Ethiopians. God responded by completely annihilating the Ethiopians such that *"none of them were left alive."* [7]

God gave King Asa a great victory. Years later, in King Asa's thirty-fifth year as king (when he is supposedly much wiser and experienced), his nation was invaded by another army. However this time King Asa did not seek the Lord's help but relied on himself. He paid off another army to team up with him and join him in battle against his invaders. His "plan" seemed to have worked but God later warned and rebuked him saying:

> *Because you have relied on the king of Syria, and have not relied on Jehovah your God, therefore the army of the king of Syria has escaped out of your hand. Were not the Cushites and the Libyans a huge army with many chariots*

and horsemen? Yet, because you relied on Jehovah, he delivered them into your hand. ⁸

But King Asa was un-repentant, to the point where the Bible states, *"Asa was diseased in his feet, until his disease was very grievous. Yet in his disease he did not seek to Jehovah, but to the physicians."* ⁹ What a sad ending to a great man. King Asa stopped making requests to God, but become self-reliant. We must not be like King Asa in his old age—in our relationship with God, we must be the lesser and weaker. In our weakness, God makes us perfect.

Jesus teaches us that in our petitions and supplications we need to be *specific* to the things we are asking for. We see that with blind Bartimeus in the book of Mark:

> *And they came to Jericho. And as He with His disciples and a large crowd went out of Jericho, blind Bartimeus, the son of Timeus, was sitting by the side of the highway, begging. And when he heard that it was Jesus of Nazareth, he began to cry out and say, 'Jesus, son of David, have mercy on me'...And Jesus stood still and commanded him to be called. And they called the blind man, saying to him, 'Be of good comfort; rise up, He is calling you.' And casting away his garment, he rose up and came to Jesus. And answering Jesus said to him, 'What do you desire that I should do to you?' The blind man said to Him, 'My Lord that I may see again.' And Jesus said to him, 'Go, your faith has healed you.' And instantly he saw again, and he followed Jesus in the way.* ¹⁰

Jesus was not oblivious to the fact that Wartimes was blind. Everyone could see that his cries were for his sight. But Jesus, still asks, *"What do you desire that I should do to you?"* God is not blind or dumb. He sees and knows your needs. But He still wants you to verbalize and make your *"requests known to Him."* [11] When we do this, we glorify Him, because when our answers come we know that it was Him who did it and not another.

Blessing Prayer

Everybody loves blessings. Every time I am ministering in my local church, and I say, "...whoever wants this blessing, run up to the altar..." before the words come out of my mouth, there is a stampede of bodies jostling to get blessed. The fact is, you don't have to wait for me or any other man of God to receive blessing. As long as you have a mouth, you can pronounce blessing. You pronounce blessings on every aspect of your life. Bless God, bless the Church, bless your pastors, bless your family, bless your President and even bless your enemies.

When you wake up in the morning, bless your spouse; tell them that this day is their day. Bless your children as they go to school. I never go or do anything minor or major without my husband blessing me. There are too many Christians out there who are running around without commanding God's blessings into their day.

When you are blessed, you cannot be cursed. Balak repeatedly offered Balaam huge sums of money if he would curse the children of Israel. He spoke to Balaam, *"saying, Come, curse Jacob for me, and come, defy Israel."* [1] Balaam prayed three times but each time, he tried to show Balak that his request was not possible saying, *"Behold, I have received word to bless. And He has blessed, and I cannot reverse it. He has not seen iniquity in Jacob, neither has He seen perverseness in Israel. Jehovah his God is with him, and the shout of a king among them."* [2] WOW, no one can remove God's blessing on our lives. No one! No witchdoctor, no wizard, no power can reverse the blessing of God on your life. The only person who can reverse the blessing of God on your life is you—by falling back into iniquity and breaking the covenant you have with Him.

This scriptural truth should set you free from living in fear of witchcraft and the occult. It should set you free from low self-worth coming from your boss or father constantly speaking word curses over you. In Africa especially, many Christian live in dread of being cursed by witchdoctors. Brothers and sisters, if you are blessed, people can hire the most powerful witchdoctor from the mountains of Tanzania; the witchdoctor can dance around his fire and throw chicken bones all night—no curse shall alight upon you. You should constantly pray blessings to reinforce the blessing you have in Christ Jesus.

 *You should constantly pray blessings to reinforce the blessing you have in Christ Jesus.*

If you are a father, the prayer of blessing over your children is probably one of the most significant things you can do for the next generation. Even God the Father, blessed His Son—the Lord Jesus Christ, saying, *"You are my Son; the Beloved, Iam delighted in You."* [3] Jacob also blessed each of his sons and some of his grandchildren before he died. The blessings he prayed went on to shape the destinies of twelve tribes of Israel. We too can shape the destinies of our lives and the lives of others.

Confession of Sins

King David was a truly a great man—a man whom God called a *"man after His heart."* [1] We all know all of the great conquests of David—how he slew Goliath, how God delivered him out of the most severest of persecutions, and how God took him from being a shepherd boy to being king of Israel. However in all this, King David was not perfect. We also know of his weaknesses and failures. We know of his infidelity with a married woman, we know of his deceit and cold-blooded murder and we know of his insecurities as a father.

We can see that even though David was imperfect God still used him greatly. And this was mainly because King David always made prayers of confessions every time he fell short of God's standard. In confession of his sins, David told God with his mouth of his failures. These prayers are so important, because they restore relationship with God and reconcile us back to Him. Let us look at one of David's confessions:

> *Have mercy on me, O God, according to Your loving-kindness; according to the multitude of Your tender mercies, blot out my transgressions. Wash me completely from my iniquity, and cleanse me from my sin. For I confess my transgressions; and my sin is ever before me. Against You, You only, have I sinned, and done evil in Your sight, that You might be justified when You speak, and be clear when You judge. Behold, I was brought forth in iniquity, and in sin did my mother conceive me. Behold, You desire truth in the inward parts; and in the hidden part You shall make me to know wisdom. Purge me with hyssop, and I*

shall be clean; wash me, and I shall be whiter than snow. Make me to hear joy and gladness; that the bones which You have broken may rejoice. Hide Your face from my sins, and blot out all my iniquities. Create in me a clean heart, 0 God, and renew a right spirit within me. Cast me not away from Your presence, and take not Your Holy Spirit. from me. Restore to me the joy of Your salvation, and uphold me with a willing spirit. [2]

King David was specific in his prayer. He told God what he did and acknowledged his failures.

We must seek and desire to be clean before Him.

We too as believers must have the same attitude as David. We must seek and desire to be clean before Him. David said in the Psalms, *"Who shall go up into the hill of Jehovah? Or who shall stand in His holy place? He who has clean hands and a pure heart; who has not lifted up his soul to vanity, and has not sworn deceitfully."* [3] God commands us, *"Be holy, for I am holy."* [4] The prayer of confession returns us to holiness and cleanses us to be "acceptable" before Him.

As Christians we have all prayed this prayer at least once—when we asked Jesus Christ to be our Lord and Savior. But I encourage you to always be quick to confess to God when you fall, and to ask Him to restore you to right standing with Him. Many Christians do not pray this prayer because of pride and at times they are not ready to live a life worthy of His name, but rather live according to their lusts.

Confession of the Word (Kaleo)

I am not a great fan of wildlife, but I am fascinated at the amazing abilities that God has given to all His creatures. One of the fastest birds alive is the peregrine falcon. When a falcon spots prey from the skies it soars to a great height and then stoops and goes into its hunting dive, diving steeply at speeds commonly said to be over 320 km/h (200 mph). Obviously, the prey of the falcon will not be stationary but moving, so the falcon is constantly changing directions at speeds over 320km/h as it homes in onto its target. Most species (and even cars and planes) cannot maneuver in this way. However, the peregrine falcon can achieve this feat easily by *slightly changing* its wing position. A *small variation* in its wing position results in a significant change in flight pattern. In fact, the greater the speed, the smaller the variation in wing position required to change direction. At times you cannot see this variation with the naked eye—all you see is a bird that has a high success rate in knocking out fast moving targets.

You might be thinking: what in the world does a peregrine falcon have to do with my prayer life?! Everything, I say. We too, as believers have a small ingredient in our arsenal that can significantly alter our life patterns. This *"small ingredient"* is our tongue. The tongue is less than 1% of the body mass in an average human yet it is the reason that wars are started and ended. It is responsible for love, for fights, for blessing and for cursing. We also use our tongue to make confession and declaration of His Word. We tell God with our mouth what He has said in His Word. We remind Him what His Word says about our current situation. Psalms 119:49 says it perfectly, *"Remember the Word to Your servant, on which You have caused me to hope."*

What we say with our tongue is so influential—death and life are in the power of the tongue.[1] James recognized the power of the tongue saying:

> *Behold, we put bits in the horses' mouths, so that they may obey us, and we turn about their whole body. Behold also the ships being so great, and driven by fierce winds, yet they are turned about with a very small rudder, where the impulse of him steering desires. Even so the tongue is a little member and boasts great things. Behold how little a fire kindles how large a forest!* [2]

 *We should confess what His Word says we are.*

By confessing His Word over your situation, you are speaking your way out of the negative and into the positive. That's why we sing, "let the weak SAY, I am strong and let the poor SAY, I am rich." We should confess what His Word says we are. Any time, we fmd ourselves in situations that are contrary to God's Word, it is a time to confess what His Word says. King David said it like this, *"With my lips I have declared all the judgments of Your mouth."* [3] Every time we confess His Word, God will not, ever, ever, without a doubt, allow His Word to return to Him void. His Word will return to Him when it has fulfilled its purpose.[4]

Declaration Prayer

Today, I am the product of the words I have declared and others have declared over my life. The fruit of my life, the things I have achieved are a result of declarations made—some of these declarations were made even before I was born. God's word endures forever[1] and any words spoken over you under the unction of the Holy Spirit will surely come to pass, even if these words were spoken hundreds of years before you were born.

 *I am the product of the words I have declared and others have declared over my life.*

Declarations are prophetic in nature because when you make declarations, you are speaking of things that are not as if they are.[2] When God declared, *"Let there be light!"*[3] light came into existence. He also spoke into being the heavens, the waters, and the whole earth as we know it today. Declarations are a statement of faith and have the power to create, to call into being, to cast out and to shift things.

Declarations are a unique type of prayer because our words are not directed at God but directed at principalities and strongholds. Jesus taught us saying, *"For truly I say to you that whoever shall say to this mountain, 'Be moved and be cast into the sea,' and shall not doubt in his heart, but shall believe that what he said shall occur, he shall have whatever he said."*[4] That is why when we pray for the sick we do not pray, "God please help this man to walk again." No, we pray, "In the name of Jesus Christ, get up and walk." We are speaking to the situation in the name of Jesus Christ. Sometimes as Christians, we need to stop pleading and making requests to God and start declaring and commanding. We have the authority. The Bible says we are gods.[5] At Creation, God clearly handed His authority to us and told us to rule and reign here on earth.[6] As gods and kings here on earth—the principalities and strongholds will obey us when we make declarations in His name.

Many Pentecostal and evangelical Christians believe this principle and utilize the type of prayer in their lives. However, there are still many believers who feel this manner of prayer is arrogant and should not be done. This group of Christians believes that only God Himself can speak in such an authoritative way—that only God can send, cast out, command the mountains and seas. Even the Pharisees and the Sadducees were offended when Jesus spoke and prayed in such a manner. I want you to understand that we are co-heirs with Christ and that we are His ambassadors on earth. As His ambassadors we have the authority to speak on behalf of His Kingdom. To give an illustration—as a Zimbabwean, if I had to go the President of South Africa in my own personal capacity and make demands of them, they will most probably not take me seriously. But if I went as an ambassador and representative of the nation of Zimbabwe, the whole weight and force of a nation is behind me. When they speak to me, they know that they are not speaking to an individual but to a whole nation. I have so much authority in this position. So, also as Christians, when we make declarations in His name, the devils and demons and strongholds know that they are not dealing with an individual but the whole of heaven. They will have no option but to obey you because they know the armies of heaven are behind you. The Proverbs say, *"Three things are stately in procession, four which are stately in their gait: The lion, mighty among the beasts, retreats before nothing. The strutting rooster, as well as the goat, and a king with his army."*[7] We are kings and we have an army behind us; we can boldly declare to the Devil and his hordes to get out of our way and they will.

Making declarations also involves the process of *"binding and loosing."* When we bind things we are closing off and disallowing the power and influence of the Devil over our lives. When we loose, we are opening and allowing God's blessing to operate in our lives. Matthew 16:19 says, *"And I will give unto thee the keys of the kingdom of heaven: and whatsoever thou shalt bind on earth shall be bound in heaven: and whatsoever thou shalt loose on earth shall be loosed in heaven."* This is repeated again in Mathew 18:18, *"Verily I say unto you, Whatsoever ye shall bind on earth shall be bound in heaven: and whatsoever ye shall loose on earth shall be loosed in heaven."* God has given us so much authority on this earth through our words; it is amazing what we can achieve with our tongue.

PART ONE — TYPES OF PRAYER

Decrees

Decrees and declarations go hand in hand at times and are very similar. While declarations are mostly prophetic, decrees are both prophetic and apostolic in nature. As mentioned in the previous section, we as Christians are gods and kings and only kings and rulers can make decrees. Two special unique qualities of decree prayers are that decrees are not reversible. Once a decree is made, even the one that made the decree cannot reverse it. I will show you patterns from the Bible in the following pages. The second thing is that when you make a decree into a domain or specific realm, people who live in or are associated with the specific domain or realm are required to live according to the dictates of the decree. Decrees affect the lives of other people—that's what makes them apostolic in nature.

 *Decrees affect the lives of other people—that's what makes them apostolic in nature.*

Now let's look at some biblical patterns of decrees. As a woman, I love Queen Esther. Her boldness and courage stirs my spirit, and I am encouraged knowing that, as Esther was, we women are nationbuilders. Now Esther lived at a time when her nation (Israel) was bound by and lived at the dictates of Persia and Medes. As we learn from the book of Esther, Haman, a man who hated the Jews and wanted to annihilate them, hatched a plan to convince the king of Persia and Medes to do so. Haman succeeded in convincing the king and the Bible says that, *"a decree was approved by the king to destroy the Jews."* [1]

We know that the king later discovers his mistake with the help of Esther and Mordecai and was outraged by Haman's trickery. The king knew that the decree that was sent out before could not be reversed, but Esther did not know so she pleaded with the king saying, *"revoke (call back the decree)"* [2] sent out by Haman. She wanted the king to counteract the decree already sent but this was not possible, so the king rather instructed Esther saying, *"You yourself write a (another) decree concerning the Jews ...seal it with the king's signet; for whatever is sealed by the king's signet cannot be revoked."* [3] The second decree enabled the Jews to defend themselves against the dictates of the first decree. From this, we learn that, when we decree a thing, it is established and cannot be revoked. Job 22:28 says, *"Thou shall also decree a thing, and it shall be established unto thee: and the light shall shine upon thy ways."*

We see this pattern repeated in the days of Daniel, when King Darius is tricked into sending out a decree that banned worship of God. When King Darius discovered that this decree meant that his friend and close associate Daniel would be executed, he was *"greatly displeased with himself"* [4] and *"labored all day to release"* [5] Daniel. However he was not successful because, *"no decree which the king establishes may be changed."* [6] We can see from the two scriptural illustrations I have shown you that decrees are not just irrevocable but they also affect the lives of other people under the influence of the decree.

In our prayer lives today, this principle is important because there are some situations that will only change only if a decree is sent out into the spirit realm. For example, as a businessman, you should be making decrees into the economy and marketplace. As a pastor, your decrees should be heard in the harvest fields of neighborhoods and cities. As a mother, decrees must be made about the friends with whom our children interact and the schools they attend. Both the minor and major prophets made decrees and judgments about Judah and Israel that are recorded in the Bible, and everything they ever said and wrote down about these nations came to pass and is still coming to pass. No one could revoke what was decreed. It was decreed by the prophets that one man would die for all mankind and when the time came for Jesus to die, not even Peter with his swash-buckling sword or the Roman legal system could stop it.

Other scriptural examples of decrees made in the Bible include:

- God decreed man shall *"till the ground"* [7] (Men today need work to earn money).

- God decreed that the woman would have pain in child bearing and that there would be enmity with mankind and the snake.[8]

- Joshua decreed that *"him and his household will serve the Lord."* [9]

- God decreed that He would not remove the lineage of David from His Throne.[10] (Today, you and I are His kings on earth sitting on the throne of David through Jesus Christ judging the nations).[11]

You can see from the few examples, that things decreed at the foundations of the earth still affect us today. So we too should know that the things we decree will affect the generations to come.

Directed Prevailing Prayer

In Luke 18:1–8, the Lord Jesus teaches on the importance of praying without ceasing (growing faint) through the parable of the unjust judge. In it He teaches about fervent, consistent, insistent prayer that continues until a breakthrough takes place. Persistence is a quality that is becoming rarer in this "microwave" generation. This generation believes in instant results—instant popcorn, instant pudding, and instant prayers.

In the parable that Jesus taught, we see that the widow never gave up in her requests. Even though she was treated harshly by the ruler, she never gave up. Some Christians will stop praying and give up simply because they do not see an answer to their prayers. They even make excuses for God's "failure" to answer, saying things like, "Maybe it is not God's will." Or "Maybe God's answer is no." God's answer to our prayers is always *"Yes and Amen!"* [1] As long as we are praying and asking God according to His Word and will, His answer is always *"Yes and Amen!"* If you haven't seen the answer to your prayers—keep praying. It is to God's pleasure to give us the things we ask for.[2]

 *If you haven't seen the answer to your prayers—keep praying.*

Elijah boldly declared that it would rain. This was after years of drought. So Elijah started praying for the rain:

and put his face between his knees. And he said to his

servant, Go up now, look toward the sea. And he went up and looked and said, 'There is nothing.' And seven times he said, 'Go again.' And it happened at the seventh time, he said, 'Behold, there arises a little cloud out of the sea, like a man's hand.' [3]

How many of us will after praying and seeing that *"there is nothing,"* will continue praying and how many of us will *"go again"* to see if our prayers are answered? If you have been praying and have not seen the manifestations of your prayer, I encourage you to be like Elijah and to *"go again"*—keep praying. Let us be like Anna, the prophetess, and Simeon who prayed for years until they had seen the Son of God manifested in the flesh.[4]

Hebrews encourages us saying, *"through faith and patience,"* [5] we will inherit the promise. We must be patient until we see our answers in the flesh. God is faithful. Do not be sluggish and draw back:

> *and do not cast away your confidence which has great reward, but you have need of endurance, so that you may receive the promise. For yet in a little while, God is coming, He will not delay. He is never late'. But you must live by faith. If you draw back, God will have no pleasure in you.* [6]

But I know that you will not draw back but you keep praying until you see His salvation in your life.

Shouting/Yelling Prayer

Samuel was a prophet and a judge in Israel. He lived in a time when *"the Word of the Lord was rare."* [1] The nation was in a bad state. The church was falling apart, the country was constantly at war and the people lived in fear. I know of countries today that are in similar positions. The Philistines were the sworn enemies of the children of Israel and were determined to crush them in battle. So the Philistines *"put themselves in battle array against Israel"* and killed over 4000 Israelis. With their backs against the wall, the Israelis turned back to the church in the hope that God will save them. So they brought the Ark of the Covenant into their camp and when the ark came in:

> *all Israel shouted so loudly that the whole earth shook. And when the Philistines heard the noise of the shout, they said, 'What is the noise of this great shout in the camp of the Hebrews? And they saw that the ark of Jehovah had come into the camp. And the Philistines were afraid, for they said, God has come into the camp, And they said, Woe to us! For there has not been a thing like this before. Woe to us! Who shall deliver us out of the hand of these mighty gods? These are the gods that struck the Egyptians with all the plagues in the wildernesses.* [2]

Firstly, from this passage of scripture, we learn that when we shout and yell in our prayers, our shouts ring across the whole earth. In the spirit realm our shout is amplified to reach the four corners of earth. Secondly, we learn that the enemy hears this shout and becomes very afraid. The devils and demons tremble at the sound of your shout. They know that their time is up.

PART ONE — TYPES OF PRAYER

Joshua was the leader of the Israelis hundreds of years earlier. He was given the mandate to lead his nation into the Promised Land. Their first challenge and test was the *small matter* of the city of Jericho. According to historians, Jericho, from a military viewpoint was almost impossible to penetrate because of the height and strength of its walls. The Bible described it as being *"tightly shut up."* [3] Historians record:

> *The most striking aspect of this early town was a massive stone wall over 3.6m high, and 1.8m wide at the base. Inside this wall was a tower over 3.6m high which contained an internal staircase with twenty-two stone steps. The wall and tower were unprecedented in human history, and would take more than 100 men, more than 100 days to construct.* [4]

This wall was at that time the cutting edge technology in military defense systems. However, as we know the best technology is no match for God. Scripture tell us how this massive wall fell:

> *And it came to pass at the seventh time, when the priests blew with the trumpets, Joshua said unto the people, Shout; for the LORD hath given you the city. So the people shouted when the priests blew with the trumpets: and it came to pass, when the people heard the sound of the trumpet, and the people shouted with a great shout, that the wall fell down flat, so that the people went up into the city, every man straight before him, and they took the city.* [5]

 *The devil wants you to be quiet and dignified in your prayers—he knows the power of your shout!*

When the Holy Spirit prompts you to shout in your prayers, know that God is about to do an unprecedented thing in your life. That is why the devil wants you to be quiet and dignified in your prayers—he knows the power of your shout. There is a roar inside each and every one of us. This roar wants to come out. The Bible describes Jesus as the Lion of Judah. A lion roars to let members of his kingdom know that there is only one king in the jungle. We too must shout and roar to let the devil know that there is only one King in this Kingdom!

PART ONE — TYPES OF PRAYER

Metaphoric Prayer

Let us talk about Joshua again; this time as a younger man under the cover of Moses. The nation of Israel had just come out of Egypt and was in the wilderness. Many of the Israelis were probably on survival mode—where getting enough water and food for the day was the main objective. The leaders were also under immense pressure with the load of leading twelve million people through the desert. We read from the Bible that there was a lot of restructuring and organizing of the leadership and governance systems.

In essence, the nation of Israel was struggling to adjust to this life in the wilderness. They did not need another issue to deal with—to be attacked by another nation—the nation of Amalek. Remember Israel did not have an army or any military experience. I wonder how many of you have ever thought you have hit rock bottom and that it cannot get any worse. The moment you think that, something worse comes along. The pit gets deeper. This is how Israel probably felt. Hunger, thirst, confusion, heat—now war!

I am sure you now can see how desperate the situation was. If we lived in those days, we would have overheard Moses talking to Joshua saying, "Joshua, Amalek is coming. Pick men who can fight and go and fight. I am going up that hill to pray." Joshua dutifully replied, "Yes sir." But he knew too well that his army would most probably get a "licking" from the highly skilled and experienced Amalek. What happened next is a demonstration of the power of what I call metaphoric prayer:

> *...And Moses, Aaron, and Hur went up to the top of the hill. And it happened when Moses held up his hand,*

> *Israel prevailed. And when he let down his hand, Amalek prevailed. But Moses' hands became heavy. And they took a stone and put it under him, and he sat on it. And Aaron and Hur held up his hands, the one on the one side, and the other on the other side. And his hands were steady until the going of the sun. And Joshua defeated Amalek and his people by the edge of the sword.* [1]

Metaphoric prayer is when symbols such as national flags, swords, or body gestures and movements are used in prayer. When Moses had his hands up, Israel prevailed; when they were down, Amalek prevailed. The Bible repeatedly talks about gateways and doorways; we need to know that our bodies and objects around us may be gateways into or out of another dimension. The Holy Spirit will lead us and reveal to us how we can use our bodies and physical objects in our prayers. When He does, be sensitive, for He is bringing victory into your life. I have been to many prayer meetings where the saints will wave specifically colored banners or dance and move in a certain way—all this is God using our metaphoric prayers to give us the victory that glorifies him. Psalms 144:1 says, *"Blessed be the LORD my strength, which teaches my hands to war, and my fingers to fight."*

PART ONE — TYPES OF PRAYER

Demonstration or Dedication Prayer

Deuteronomy 20:5 states, *"And the officers shall speak to the people saying, Who is the man that has built a new house and has not dedicated it? Let him go and return to his house, lest he die in the battle and another man dedicate it."* The fact is, there are things dedicated to God. The Bible records how Moses through the Law, gave instructions to the children of Israel on how they could dedicate their houses, possessions and even sons, to the Lord. Even though dedication instructions were given through the Law, dedication is still a spiritual principle that applies to us today who live under Grace. The methods and means are different from the Old Testament, but the fact remains that as mature Christians, dedication of our possessions should be a lifestyle.

Today, we can dedicate our possessions by driving stakes in land we have just purchased; pouring oil, sprinkling dirt, sprinkling salt, or pouring water are other methods that the Holy Spirit has revealed to the church on how to dedicate things to the Lord. We as a church decided that we needed to place strategic proclamations throughout the city to dedicate the city to God. We have encouraged our congregation to place bottles of oil around the altar during preaching or to bring soil from their particular communities so that the oil and soil are cleansed and sanctified by His Word. The oil or soil can then be taken back to their communities or domains to be used to dedicate an item or community to God.

Now, stakes, oil, soil, salt or any other dedication items have no power in themselves but the power comes when we pray and dedicate the items for specific purpose. We do not worship creation but we worship the Creator.¹ When we pray these prayers, we know His Power will come upon what we are dedicating.

 *Some of the evil and vile things that are happening in our lives are a result of the possessions we have that are still dedicated to the devil.*

So, I encourage you, if you have just checked into a hotel room, pray for it and dedicate it to Him, because you do not know what the previous guest did. When you buy land, you do not know if it has being given to the occult or not—so drive a stake into the ground, then pray and commit the land to God. For all your possessions, do this. Do not take things for granted! King David did not take things for granted. All the spoils of war, he won, he dedicated to the house of God. Some of the evil and vile things that are happening in our lives are a result of the possessions we have that are still dedicated to the devil, hence there is a curse attached to them. Ask the Holy Spirit to help you in this area and seek His wisdom on the power of dedication prayers.

PART ONE — TYPES OF PRAYER

Sacks and Ashes Prayer

The prayer of "sacks and ashes" is more of a *disposition* or condition of the heart during prayer. In the Old Testament, when, *"...the children of Israel were assembled with fasting, and with sack clothes, and earth upon the,"* [1] it was usually a time of great distress or repentance. We see numerous times in the Old Testament, when kings and the people of God, would put on sackcloth and dust when they realized that they needed God to intervene immediately. In 2 Kings 19:1, we read about King Hezekiah, *"And it came to pass, when king Hezekiah heard it, that he rent his clothes, and covered himself with sackcloth, and went into the house of the LORD."* In 1 Kings 21:27–29 we also read about how King Ahab repented:

> *And it came to pass, when Ahab heard those words, that he rent his clothes, and put sackcloth upon his flesh, and fasted, and lay in sackcloth, and went softly. The word of the LORD came to Elijah the Tishbite, saying, 'See how Ahab humbles himself before me? Because he humbles himself before me, I will not bring the evil in his days: but in his son's days will I bring the evil upon his house.'*

Despite these two kings being in two different circumstances, their hearts were in a state of brokenness and contriteness. Our prayers are like sweet-smelling incense to God's nostrils when we pray in humbleness and contriteness.[2] Hezekiah had the largest army in the world (at that time) sitting at his gates waiting to invade and Ahab was an accessory to the murder of an innocent man. Both men were in severe distress and needed immediate intervention from God. Both men humbled themselves and God lifted them out of their pits.

We too when faced with an "enemy sitting at our gates" ready to devour us, must humble ourselves and seek His salvation in the situation. Today, when we pray like this, we don't rent our clothes and throw dust on our heads—if you did that, you would be thrown in a psych ward. Rather the Bible says, *"when you fast, anoint your head and wash your face, so that you do not appear to men to fast, but to your Father in secret. And your Father who sees in secret shall reward you openly."* [3] It is not about the outward appearance but the inward condition of your heart. These are "do or die" prayers—if God does not do something, then there is going to be a major disaster.

 *Sacks and ashes prayers are "do or die" prayers—if God does not do something, then there is going to be a major disaster.*

Be encouraged in the knowledge that when you humble yourself in "sackcloth and ashes", he will lift you out of the situation you are in.

PART ONE — TYPES OF PRAYER

Praying In the Spirit

Out of our bellies flows a river of the Holy Spirit.[1] This river brings life and healing to the nations.

> *...When this river reaches the sea, its waters are healed. And it shall be that every living thing that moves, wherever the river goes shall live. There will be a multitude of fish, because these waters got here; for there will be healed, and everything will live wherever the river goes...Along the bank of the river, on this side and that, will grow all kinds of trees used for food; their leaves will not wither, and their fruit will not fail. They will bear fruit every month, because their water flows from the sanctuary. Their fruit will be for food and their leaves for medicine.* [2]

This river is the river of the Spirit and this river flows when we pray in the Spirit. The Bible describes this as praying in tongues—it is praying in the language of heaven. If you have situations around you that are dead and sick, pray in the Spirit, because when the waters of the Spirit come into contact with dead situations they will bring healing and life.

Now the waters of a river do not stop flowing. Day in, day out, they do not cease. This is why Paul says, *"pray without ceasing"* [3] You can pray without ceasing in the Spirit because when you pray in the Spirit, you are not using your mind but the Spirit is giving you the utterance, so you will never run out of words to pray. I am always praying under my breath—even when I am driving or cooking; I pray continuously. My spirit is always rumbling and bubbling with words from heaven. Now, I want you to imagine you are a farmer. Your three main ingredients for farming are water, seed and soil. Now if the ground is hard, you will have to water the ground to soften it, in order to plough. The ground of our lives has to be watered by the waters of the Spirit, so that the seed, which is the spoken Word, may be sown. Praying in the Spirit softens our hearts and prepares us to receive His Word. His Word gives us faith, that's why Jude says, *"But ye, beloved, building up yourselves on your most holy faith, praying in the Holy Ghost."*

 *My spirit is always rumbling and bubbling with words from heaven.*

Praying in tongues is a powerful way to engage in prayer. When you shut everything else out and let tongues flow from you like a river, you move from ankle deep prayer into flowing waters deep enough for swimming.

PART ONE — TYPES OF PRAYER

Concert Prayer

Two is better than one. One Christian can put a thousand demons to flight and two Christians can set legions of demons fleeing.[1] The prayer of agreement is powerful because Jesus said to us, *"...at the mouth of two or three witnesses every word is established,"*[2] I believe in the concept of "prayer partners." You should have someone in your life who you call on at any given moment to stand with you in agreement. Even Jesus, needed prayer partners, when he said to Peter, James and John, *"come pray with me."*[3] Paul also said to his church, *"But I exhort you, brothers, for the sake of the Lord Jesus Christ and for the love of the Spirit, that you strive together with me in your prayers to God for me."*[4] Both Jesus and Paul desired that Christians pray together in agreement, because they understood that, for some situations to change, "concert prayers" were needed.

The Bible records numerous times when the children of Israel would gather together to pray. The Bible also records how the early church also gathered regularly to pray together—sometimes even at the risk of imprisonment. They too understood the power of agreement. Today, as a church, we should be making every effort to meet together to pray. At our church in Harare, we have set aside times where members of the church come together and pray. These "concert prayers" are so important, especially when praying for issues of national or regional significance. I know of Christians who do not attend prayer meetings, but have private "closet" prayer times alone. I also know of Christians who attend prayer meetings but do not have private prayer time with the Lord. As Christians, we need to practice both lifestyles. Balance is the key to life.[5] If you practice one and not the other, you are out of balance and are not living in the fullness of Christ.

 *Today, as a church, we should be making every effort to meet together to pray.*

We should also pray with our spouses and children. Praying together regularly with your spouse or children builds intimacy. Some authors have proven that couples that pray together have a better sex-life than those that do not.[6] They also show that parents that pray with their children have closer relationships with their children than parents that do not. I encourage you to gather together with other believers and join your voice with the voices of other believers, and together our voice will bring His Kingdom here on earth.

PART ONE — TYPES OF PRAYER

Spiritual Warfare Prayer

Now ALL prayers are warfare. Whether you are praying in tongues, or declaring, decreeing or in thanksgiving—all manner of prayer is warfare. 2 Corinthians 10:3–5 shows this saying:

> *For though we walk in the flesh, we do not war after the flesh: (For the weapons of our warfare are not carnal, but mighty through God to the pulling down of strong holds;) Casting down imaginations, and every high thing that exalteth itself against the knowledge of God, and bringing into captivity every thought to the obedience of Christ.*

Again Ephesians 6:12 says, *"For we wrestle not against flesh and blood, but against principalities, against powers, against the rulers of the darkness of this world, against spiritual wickedness in high places."*

Having said this, I want to bring emphasis to specific warfare prayers I believe that all Christians will face at some point of their journey with the Lord. This warfare prayer is first seen in the book of Daniel when the angel Gabriel has this conversation with Daniel:

> *And he said to me, 'O Daniel, a man greatly beloved, understand the words that I speak to you, and stand upright. For to you I am now sent.' And when he had spoken this word to me, I stood trembling. Then he said to me, 'Do not fear, Daniel; for from the first day that you set your heart to understand and to chasten yourself before your God, your words were heard. And I have come for your words. But the ruler of the kingdom of Persia*

withstood me twenty-one days. But lo, Michael, one of the chief rulers, came to help me; and I remained there with the kings of Persia.' [1]

Daniel had prayed, and his prayers were heard in heaven and heaven responded to him, but the response could NOT get back to him because Satan had directly withstood Gabriel. There are times when Satan will not be subtle or cunning in his approach but he will directly oppose you face to face. These are times, as in Daniel's case, where you need Michael—the commander of God's armies to war on your behalf.

We see a glimpse of this war in Revelation 12:7–9:

And there was war in heaven: Michael and his angels fought against the dragon; and the dragon fought and his angels, and prevailed not; neither was their place found any more in heaven. And the great dragon was cast out, that old serpent, called the Devil, and Satan, which deceives the whole world: he was cast out into the earth, and his angels were cast out with him.

Again, we see this direct confrontation with Paul when he says to the Thessalonians, *"...Satan has hindered us."* [2] As Christians, we must know and have the discernment to know when Satan has come to hinder us or withhold our prayers.

When we know this, as we pray, we know that Michael and his angels are fighting and prevailing on our behalf. Usually, this kind of open warfare is seen when our capacities are being enlarged. When your business is expanding to a new sales region; or your church is taking the gospel to a new unreached territory, you will find that Satan will come out against you to oppose you in your face. But be encouraged in the knowledge that Satan is defeated already and that he will lose every battle that he fights against you.

 *These are prayers where our countenance is fierce.*

In our church, sometimes, when we are faced with open warfare from the Evil One, we pray what we call Power Prayers and Ramming Speed Prayers. These are prayers where our countenance is fierce. We are warriors in battles. Our body language is aggressive and our voices are authoritative. The Bible describes this countenance and disposition in 1 Chronicles 12:8 saying, *"And of the Gadites there separated themselves unto David to the stronghold in the wilderness, mighty men of valor, men trained for war, that could handle shield and spear; whose faces were like the faces of lions, and they were as swift as the roes upon the mountains."* During Power Prayers and Ramming Speed Prayers, the devil sees our faces as lions. He is afraid of lions, because lions remind him of the Lion of Judah. In my life I know that I will fight many of these battles, but I am confident of victory because He who leads me into battle is the Lord of Lords.

Meditation

I have spoken a great deal regarding prayers that involve using our mouths. I also mentioned that we can use our bodies as an expression of prayer. But God has given us a heart to use in prayer as well; we can pray with our hearts. In fact, prayers of the heart are some of the purist and life-changing prayers we can pray. Because they are unspoken, they come from the deepest part of our hearts straight into God's heart. God sees and hears everything that we "speak" with our hearts. David says, *"Let the words of my mouth, and the meditation of my heart, be acceptable in thy sight, 0 LORD, my strength, and my redeemer."* [1]

When we deliberately and purposively reflect on the word of God it brings success and prosperity to us. We saw this with Joshua, when God told him, *"This book of the law shall not depart out of thy mouth;* **but thou shalt meditate therein day and night**, *that thou may observe to do according to all that is written therein: for then thou shalt make thy way prosperous, and then thou shalt have good success."* [2] During this time of prayer it is a good idea to keep a pen and writing pad close to you. It is in meditative prayer that we usually hear God speak to us specifically about certain issues or He gives us promises, solutions and answers. Prayer is communication with God, and communication is two way. Many Christians speak a lot but they do not stop speaking to hear what God is saying. If God commands us to "pray without ceasing," [3] it means He also speaks back to us without ceasing. Meditation prayer should be engaged in while we are having our alone time with God. God wants us to separate ourselves so that we concentrate on Him and He can engage us without interruption. These truly are powerful times. Our hunger and thirst for Him should be heightened and our passion can be poured out in response to our yielding to His voice.

 *The church today, needs more Marys and fewer Marthas.*

I know of Christians today who cannot have a quiet moment with themselves, even for a minute. They are always doing something—in meetings, running around and arranging something "important." Even when alone, they are texting, facebooking or tweeting. Jesus says we must be like Mary, *"and sit at the feet of Jesus."* [4] The church today, needs more Marys and fewer Marthas. David and Joshua got their strength during these quiet times. Sometimes my husband, who is usually chatty and has a thing or two to say about everything, will suddenly go quiet. During these moments, I have learnt not to disturb him because I know he is in a moment of meditation, and God is downloading His truth into his heart. We need to be more like my husband and use our hearts and minds to reach out to Him.

Weeping Prayer

Big boys don't cry! If you are telling this to your sons, you are setting them up for failure. *Jesus wept.*[1] King David on numerous times sobbed liked a baby. Both these men were two of the greatest men that ever walked this earth—and they wept in public. Today, men cannot be seen weeping. They must be seen macho and strong. What a lie from the pits of hell. The Bible clearly says, *"...in your weakness, My strength is made perfect."*[2] When we confess and show God that we are unable and powerless, He makes us able and makes us strong. Psalms 126:5–6 says, *"They that sow in tears shall reap in joy. He that goes forth weeping, bearing precious seed, shall doubtless come again with rejoicing, bringing his sheaves with him."*

We must remember that weeping keeps us tender and sensitive to God's spirit. Weeping prayers are effective when we cry out to God from a deep sense of anguish or pain. Sometimes our words cannot express the emotional stress we are under and so weeping helps us to express our feelings in a way that only He understands. Weeping prayers are prayers from the soul.

When you are weeping you are showing God how vulnerable you are. All your emotional guards are off and you are allowing God to go all the way into your heart. The measure you allow God into your heart is the measure He allows you into His heart. The Bible says it this way, *"Draw near to Me, and I will draw near to you..."*[3] Unfortunately, when we are in control of our emotions, we are also in clear control of how much of God we can let into our situation. However, during weeping, all these defenses are down and God will come in like a flood.

 *Weeping lasts for a season.*

We can be assured that weeping lasts for a season only—our joy and salvation comes in the morning. You will not weep forever. You may be grieved and sorrowful now, but I know that soon you will be filled in His joy and gladness.

Apostolic Rank Prayer

We are all equal in Christ but we are all not equal in His Government. In His Government, we are of different ranks and positions. Some have been given much.[1] Some have been given hundred-fold, others sixty-fold and yet others thirty-fold.[2] Some have been given *five* talents, others two talents and yet others one talent.[3] We are all of different ranks. The Bible shows us this saying, *"All these were men of war, keeping rank, they came with a perfect heart to Hebron..."* [4] and again saying, *"They shall run like mighty ones. They shall climb the wall like men of war, and they shall march each one on his way, and they shall not break their ranks."* [5]

 *We are all equal in Christ but we are all not equal in His Government.*

Apostolic declarations or rank prayers are a type of prayer prayed by believers of higher rank over believers and situations of lower rank. These are the prayers prayed by the elders of the church. The Bible has many examples of these including James saying, *"Is any sick among you? Let him call for the elders of the church, and let them pray over him, anointing him with oil in the name of the Lord."* [6] Paul also indicates this saying, *"Do not neglect the gift in you, which was given you by prophecy, with the laying on of the hands of the body of elders"* [7]

This is why when we take an offering, or first-fruit to our man of God, you must ask him to pray for you because the blessing he pronounces over you is irrevocable. You can pray and fast for the rest of your life, but if you do not have the blessing and endorsement from your man of God, you will not live to the fullest potential of your life.

 *We must always seek and covet the prayers and blessing of our elders.*

In our churches today, there are cases of "empty hands laying hands on empty heads." We must always seek and covet the prayers and blessing of our elders. Job's three friends would have perished without Job praying for them. The nation of Israel would have perished in the wilderness without Moses praying for them. We too will perish, if our elders do not pray for us and bless us.

Prophetic Prayer

Prophecy has always been an enigmatic topic over the generations. Many religions, cults and occults all desire to prophesy and see into the future. Non-believers want to see into the future because of fear of the unknown. As Christians, we do not fear the unknown, but rather God has given us the gift of prophecy so we can, *"build, exhort and comfort"* [1] each other as believers. *"He that prophesies builds up the church."* [2] Our prophecies build up the body of Christ as a whole. It makes the church stronger; it gives the church direction and purpose. Moses spoke to Joshua saying, *"...if only all God's people were prophets."* [3] God greatly desires that we prophesy because He clearly says, *"I will not do anything unless I reveal it to the prophets first."* [4] Sometimes we hinder and frustrate the works of God because of the lack of prophetic voice in our lives.

 *Non-believers want to see into the future because of fear of the unknown.*

All prophecies are inspired by the Holy Spirit and line up with the Scriptures. If a prophetic prayer word does not line up with the Scriptures, it is not from God but from deceiving spirits, whose intention is to break up the church. Today, the church is so torn apart because men of God have received and accepted words from deceiving spirits. The Bible encourages us to *"test every spirit"* [6] to see if it is from God.

I love the prophetic, because with it, we see into the heart of God. We see the works He wants to do. When we prophesy over a person or situation, we see that person as God sees them or we see that situation as God sees it. Through prophesy, we have God's perspective on the issues of life. Prophetic prayer will bring our future to us. If we lift our voices and prophetically call out, we will begin to see the will of God being done here on earth.

Sacrificial Prayer

When we mix our prayers with sacrifice, we will see a dynamic response from heaven. If we as believers do not add to our prayers an offering or sacrifice that costs us something, our prayers will at times be ineffective. This is especially true when you are praying for financial breakthrough. If you want to see major breakthrough in your life—pray and give! This combination is a lethal weapon to the kingdom of darkness.

In the book of Acts, we read about a Roman soldier named Cornelius—he was *"praying continuously"* but also *"gave alms"* to the poor.[1] Because of this, an angel was sent to him saying, *"... your prayers and alms have come up before God."* [2] This passage of Scripture is of paramount importance to both you and me today, because Cornelius's prayers and giving paved the way for the gospel to be preached to the Gentiles for the very first time. It was the first time the Bible records a public ministry session to the Gentiles. Today, if you are non-Jewish and are a Christian know that it was because of Cornelius's prayers and alms that the gospel was able to go outside. Without this sacrificial prayer, many of us would not have heard the gospel, and the message of the Kingdom would be contained to the Jewish people.

If you want to see major breakthrough in your life—pray and give!

I am showing you this because I want you to see the significance of mixing our prayers with sacrifice. When King Solomon mixed his prayers with a sacrifice of bulls, it provoked God to ask him, *"Ask, what shall I give you?"* [3] King Solomon was given a blank check by God. Imagine, the Kings of Kings asking you this question. Abraham and Sarah also mixed their prayers with sacrifice when they sacrificed a young calf to the three "men" that passed by them. The result is that they declared that by this time next year, Sarah would be with child. Abraham and Sarah became parents in their nineties. I can show you over and over again in the Scriptures of how men and women of God mixed prayer and giving and you will see how God broke through for them.

If we as a church practice this principle, we will see ourselves taking our rightful places as sons of God, here on earth. The church today is weak because our giving has not exceeded the giving of the enemy. The early church gave up whole properties, livelihoods and even their own lives to see His Kingdom come. Today, our churches are in debt, our cities are filled with the poor and sick, while we Christians think we can just pray everything away. Yes, prayer is key but a cake has many ingredients, and the ingredient, I believe we should add to our prayers, is our sacrifice. Then we will see the kingdoms of this world become the kingdoms of our Lord.[4]

TEACH US TO PRAY

PART II
WHY PRAY?

Having described the different types of prayers I would like to remind you why you should always pray ALL manner of prayer. Peter said, *"Wherefore I will not be negligent to put you always in remembrance of these things, though you know them, and be established in the present truth."* [1] My desire is that I want you to always remember the weapons that God has given you for your battles here on earth. So even if you know these things and are established in them, the things of God are deep—you can never know enough. Ask and seek Him to reveal to you deeper truths about prayer.

The question I want to ask today's church is, "why do we pray?" Sounds like an inane question—but some of the responses I would get from this question would probably be more ridiculous than the question asked. Some Christians will only pray when they need God to do something for them. They pray according to their greed, so they may *"consume upon their lusts."* [2] Others pray because they have to, as a sense of duty; hence their prayers are just *"vain repetitions."* [3] If you had to record their prayers for the whole year, you will find they are saying the same things over and over again. Others pray, but their hearts are hardened and far away from God. As Christians we should not fall into any of these categories—if we do, we are simply being "religious" and missing the point of prayer.

Today the power of prayer is greatly underestimated and many believers, who do not have prayer as a lifestyle, miss out on an intimate relationship with God. There was a time, before the fall of man, before the creation of woman that the only person Adam could communicate with, was God. Can you imagine the intimacy? Can you imagine how the whole of heaven focused all its energy in one man? God's main objective for each day was to get to know Adam better and Adam's objective for each day was to learn how to communicate with God in all His different facets. Remember God has many names and many titles; the way we speak to God the Father, is not the same way we speak to the Lord of Hosts. That is why He gave us all manner of praying. With all manner of praying, we get to communicate to all His different names and titles.

A story is commonly told of a young man who wanted to move to America to build a new life there. He managed to sell all he had to just afford the lowest grade of tickets for a place on a liner ship to America. He considered that he did not have any food so he salvaged some money to buy enough cheese and crackers for the long journey. Once on the ship the young man kept to himself keeping his mind on the destination and what he wanted to achieve. So night after night the man went to sleep on a stomach filled with cheese and crackers. Three days before the journey came to an end the captain of the ship spotted the young man and asked him why he had never seen him in the banqueting room with the rest of the passengers. The young man shyly explained his dream to go to America and how he was only able to afford a ticket for board and passage but not for the food. Surprised at what he heard, the captain told the young man *"I'm saddened that you did not find this out earlier, but the ticket you bought included eating in the banquet room where you get to eat whatever you like and as much as you want!"*

PART ONE — TYPES OF PRAYER

When we limit our prayers to a certain type of prayer or a way of praying, we are like this young man. We are eating cheese and crackers when we should be feasting in the banquet room. How many believers because of their lack of prayer go through their lives living like the young man—just getting by? If you have been a Christian for a long time and live a life of just getting by—stop and look at your life. Listen to your prayers. Be humble like the disciples and ask the Lord to teach you how to pray.

Purpose in your heart to walk in the authority, power, and dominion that God has for you. Be determined to live the life that Christ desires for you and nothing less. If you live below His standard, you are doing yourself an injustice and you are doing the world an injustice.

I pray I am stoking your fire and stirring up your heart to pray. I pray this book puts a fire in your bones and zeal to pursue Him with all manner of prayer. Let us pray together as the body of Christ saying as Christ said in Matthew 6:9–13

> *Our Father, who is in Heaven, Hallowed be Your name.*
> *Your kingdom come, Your will be done, on earth as it is in Heaven.*
> *Give us this day our daily bread;*
> *And forgive us our debts as we also forgive our debtors.*
> *And lead us not into temptation, but deliver us from the evil.*
> *For Yours is the kingdom, and the power, and the glory, forever. Amen.*

Additional Notes on Prayer

Prayer affects and inspires our thoughts. It informs us of our deficiencies so that we can adjust our mindset, behavior, and character to His Word. We must bring our own mental faculties, emotions and behavior under submission to the Word of God. There is need for discipline, self-control and humility when prayer requests, intercession, petitions and supplications are made to God. Below are a few more important notes on prayer:

- Prayer provides us with understanding (Eph. 3:13–21; 6:18–19).

- Prayer is intimate fellowship that communes with God (2 Cor. 1:2–4) in worship and thankfulness (Eph. 1: 1–11).

- Prayer absorbs guidance and wisdom.

- Prayer is LIFE in God.

- Prayer is a time to obtain answers and to achieve victory (2 Cor. 2:14).

- Prayer gives us strength and heightens our expectation.

- Prayer renews our faith, hope and love.

- Prayer moves us into power, authority and dominion. The spirit and power of love and a sound mind comes on us (2 Tim. 1:7, Daniel 6:10,1 Peter 5:7–8 AMP).

PART ONE — TYPES OF PRAYER

- "A sound mind is capable of making the correct decisions as it pertains to the kingdom of God. The transformed intelligent mind is essential to victorious living."

- Prayer penetrates the spirit realm and brings manifestation that can be seen—results (Phil. 4:4–6). It gives us guidance and wisdom (1 Thes. 5:17, 18,23,24,28, James 1:5–8, 17). We governmentally decree what God has pre-ordained from eternity past (Micah 7:11, Ezra 6). We speak out the Word of God upon all situations. It is not just verbalizing to God, but also commanding the circumstances in accordance with His purposes.

- As we speak out the mind of God in prayer, He releases angels to perform invisible functions that accomplish the Word. Prayer looses God's kingdom on earth and in our lives as it is in heaven.

- Effective prayers SEE with open eyes of understanding into the spiritual realm. With creative words, we make authoritative, apostolic declarations that take ascendancy over the present system. Now, whether we pray for minutes or hours, we sense targeted victory. When we pray decisively, it's always effective.

- Prayer brings direction and releases God's timing (Matt. 24:19–21).

- Prayer creates the opportunity for us to escape the snare of the devil and for us to escape evil (Matt. 6:12, Luke 11:5–6; 21:36) and not to fall into temptation.

- Prayer moves delays and death assignments and allows prophecies and plans to come to pass (Rom. 1:10), so that the mysteries of the Kingdom of God are revealed and released (Eph. 6:19–20, Matt. 13:11–17).

- Prayer opens doors that have been shut sometimes for centuries, pulling down walls of demonic oppression and demonic possession.

- Prayer anoints messengers of the age to release the gospel with power and demonstration (Heb. 2:1–4).

- Prayer empowers the spirit of unity (John 17:20–21).

- Prayer in the spirit creates opportunities for the gifts of the Holy Spirit to manifest—such as tongues and interpretation, prophecy, word of knowledge and word of wisdom (1 Cor. 12:8–13, 1 Cor 14:13–14).

Accurate prayer is absolutely vital and ESSENTIAL. James says we have not because we ask amiss. He says that Elijah was a man of like passions and prayed that it would not rain for three and a half years, and it happened. He prayed decisively, which is imperative for the following reasons:

- Decisive prayer ploughs up new ground in preparation for the necessary Kingdom tasks. We combine forces with God to revolutionize that which He desires.

- Decisive prayer establishes God's governmental victory over regions and Nations and moves against mentalities antagonistic to God's will in the Earth. It dismantles long standing rigid mindsets.

- Decisive prayer releases God's ways of thinking and creates a Kingdom mentality. It declares His reality, order and organization over the spiritual environment that relates to our lives.

- Decisive prayer opens the door to creativity and new thought (Ps. 92:1–6).

- Decisive prayer is not begging or pleading. Prayer must not begin from weakness but must forcefully demolish old impotent ground. Anything that resists God's purpose must be torn down.

- Decisive prayer is the power of agreement that liberates and releases intentional unity in the Body of Christ (Acts 1:14; 2:1; 2:46). It then activates the Power of the Holy Spirit to be poured out.

TEACH US TO PRAY

PART III
THE HEAVENLY COURT

In this closing section, I want to paint a picture for you. Leonardo Da Vinci painted the "Last Supper",[1] depicting Jesus having his last meal with His disciples. My painting will not be on an actual canvas but rather on the canvas of your minds. My painting is of what prayer looks like. I want you to have this picture because it is essential to understand the system to which our prayers are subject. I call this picture, the Heavenly Court system.

If you were to go to any house, office or nation, you will find that each of these institutions will have a system or way of doing things. It is important to know the protocol and systems of places we interact with in order to have impact in those places. This is also true for prayer. When we enter into the Heavenly Court, we must know the protocols and systems of His Court.

The Heavenly Court System is also referred to as the Council of God. The Bible has other names for it too:

- Divine Council—Psalm 82:1
- Counsel of EI (God)—Job 15:8
- The Council of Yahweh—Jeremiah 23:18
- Council of the Holy Ones—Psalm 89:7

The Divine Council

A council is an assembly of persons summoned or convened for consultation deliberating and giving advice. It is a governing and legislative body. Sort of like a board for a business or a church committee. Hence when the Heavenly Court is in session, the members of the court form a body referred to as the Divine Council. When the members of the Divine Council convene and listen to the Lord's message and engage in discussion the members are listening to God's advice and wisdom—His divine counsel.

The divine counsel of God is described differently in several places in scripture. The heavenly courts can be found on earth or in heaven, and both the counsel and council of God are always linked to the dwelling place of God. Let us paint a picture below of the members that are present in the Divine Council.

God
God the Trinity is part of the council. That is God the Father, Christ the Son of God, and the Holy Spirit. Psalm 82:1 says *"God has taken His place in the Divine Council; in the midst of the gods he holds judgment."* God resides over the Divine Council as heavenly council and all in the council submit to Him obeying His decrees and counsel.

The Hosts of Heaven
Judges 5:20 says, *"They fought from the heavens; the stars from their courses fought against Sisera."* The hosts of heaven include: the angels; the Cherubim and the Seraphim; Michael, the archangel,

who is the leader of angels in battle and the archangel over the nation of Israel; and Gabriel, who brings interpretation of divine revelation concerning times and seasons of the church.

The Twenty-four Elders
Revelation 4:4 says, *"Twenty-four other thrones surrounded the throne and seated on these thrones were twenty-four elders arrayed in white clothing, with crowns of gold upon their heads."* The elders in attendance in the throne room of God are of high rank. Each has their own throne and crown signifying the authority they held. The elders each submit their authority to God and give honor and glory to Him.

The Cloud of Witnesses
The cloud of witnesses consists of apostles, prophets, and saints of old, whose lives are a testimony of the faithfulness and goodness of God. We see this in Scripture when Moses and Elijah met with Jesus at the Mount of Transfiguration.[2]

The Divine Council also consists of Saints, Governmental Apostles, Governmental Prophets, and Ranked Intercessors that are alive on the earth today. As Christians, we too stand in the Divine Council. That is why the Bible says, *"we will judge nations"* [3] and *"we will judge angels"* [4] and also that is why the Zebedee brothers asked Jesus, *"grant us that we sit next to you in the Kingdom of Heaven."* [5] They were asking for a seat on the Council table.

The Devil
Job 1:6 says, *"One day the angels (sons of men) came to present themselves before the Lord and Satan also came with them."* Zechariah

3:1 says *"And He showed me Joshua the high priest standing before the Angel of Jehovah, and Satan standing at his right hand to accuse him."* Satan comes to these gatherings to accuse the sons of God.

So we have seen all the different "characters" in the Council. As believers today, we can see, as part of the Council, we stand in a fearful and terrifying place. That is why when Isaiah caught a glimpse of the Council, he was overwhelmed and cried *"woe is me."* [6] John too, when he saw the Council *"fell down as dead."* [7]

When this Council has gathered, the Bible gives us a practical indication of how we can invoke the Council to meet and deliberate on our requests or in a sense compel the Council to make judgment on behalf of our nations.

The heavenly court is situated in the throne room of God. The prophet Daniel gives one of the best descriptions of the throne room to be found in scripture:

> *I watched till thrones were put in place, and the Ancient of Days was seated; His garment was white as snow, and the hair of His head was like pure wool. His throne was a fiery flame, its wheels a burning fire, a fiery stream issued and came forth from before Him. A thousand thousands ministered to Him; Ten thousand times ten thousand stood before Him. The court was seated, and the books were opened.* [8]

In the above passage, Daniel identifies the Ancient of Days as the One presiding over judgment, and the Son of Man, Jesus Christ, receiving His glorious Kingdom.

When the Council is seated, it will make judgments over the affairs of the world. We see an example of this when judgment is made over King Ahab. The Bible records Micah saying to King Ahab:

> *Therefore hear the word of the LORD: I saw the LORD sitting on His throne, and all the host of heaven standing by, on His right hand and on His left. And the LORD said, 'Who will persuade Ahab to go up, that he may fall at Ramoth Gilead?' So one spoke in this manner, and another spoke in that manner. Then a spirit came forward and stood before the LORD, and said, 'I will persuade him.' The LORD said to him, 'In what way?' So he said, 'I will go out and be a lying spirit in the mouth of all his prophets.' And the LORD said, 'You shall persuade him, and also prevail. Go out and do so.' Therefore look! The LORD has put a lying spirit in the mouth of all these prophets of yours, and the LORD has declared disaster against you.* [9]

This passage of scripture gives us a picture of a court session going on in heaven. Micah, the prophet, begins by describing the Lord sitting on His throne, surrounded by the host of heaven. We read that an evil spirit answers the Lord's question: *"Who will persuade Ahab to go up, that he may fall at Ramoth Gilead?"* The demon comes forward, replying: *"I will persuade him... I will go out and be a lying spirit in the mouth of his prophets."* Then the Lord gives permission to the evil spirit: *"You shall persuade him and also prevail. Go out and do it."*

So, even evil spirits, at times, can be a part of the Divine Council of heaven to accomplish God's will! But evil spirits don't have the last say! We have a part in judgment against our adversary the devil, who is constantly battling against prosperity coming into our lives. Although we need God to bring judgment, He invites us to be involved in the divine counsel concerning our life and death, our fate and inheritance. We also see the involvement of demonic angelic princes in the council meeting in the heavens in the book of Job, where Job becomes a discussion piece.

There are several examples of how we as Christians today can get involved in the deliberations of the Council. Abraham, in Genesis 18, intercedes as a Council Member. God appears with two angels, possibly Michael and Gabriel, to complete a business transaction with Abraham and Sarah, and seals the deal with a son—Isaac. The second order of business is Sodom and Gomorrah. In Genesis 18:22, Abraham stood before the Lord, and in verse 23 he asked, *"Will you destroy the righteous with the wicked?"* As a Council member, he had the power of veto. He could not persuade God to change His position on the twin cities. Abraham did however manage to get his nephew and family out of the cities before the judgment of God fell.

Moses intercedes as a Council Member in Numbers 14:13. Israel, as a nation, from the day of their deliverance from slavery in Egypt, complained and constantly kindled and provoked God to release His wrath and JUDGMENT.

Numbers 13 gives the commentary of events leading the spies into the promise land, and specifies the actions of the ten spies with an evil report, and the faith report of Joshua and Caleb. The people believed the ten. As seen in Numbers 14, the people wept all night and by morning decided that is was not the time to go in and possess the land. God said to Moses, step aside so that I will destroy all these people and build of you a great nation. Moses then uses his authority as a Council member to persuade God not to destroy the people. He says to God, You cannot do this as the nations around will say, *"You brought them into the wilderness to kill them."* [10] However judgment does fall on the ten spies and many that were in direct disobedience to God. From that court hearing, the ruling was that all over the age of twenty-one would not enter into the promise land (Numbers 14:29).

Acts 15 is another example of a Council meeting recorded in the Bible where the apostles confer and preside over very sensitive issues concerning the direction and the destiny of the Church. At first it was a men only meeting, until Peter when giving the final judgment, proclaims *"...it seemed good to us AND the Holy Spirit..."* [11] showing that other members of the Divine Council were present in this meeting. In this case the apostles were falling into agreement with the judgment the Holy Spirit had given.

It is of paramount importance that we understand the Heavenly throne, and the fundamental function of the Council of God. An understanding of this releases power to our prayers for our families, our ministries, our cities and nations. We can appeal to the throne of God and demand Justice (a ruling on our behalf) to change the course of action set by the demonic agenda in our lives.

Some of you are probably in shock and disbelief of how much authority you have in Christ. Why do you think David said to God, *"Why You esteem man so highly, that You made him a little lower than the angels?"* [12] God sees us fit to be part of His Council. He has allowed us to sit at His right hand and judge the nations with Him. He has made us His co-workers and we are co-heirs with His Son. So when you pray, do not pray like a "wimpy little" Christian but pray like you are the son of God with full rights to the Promise.

PART IV
EFFECTUAL FERVENT PRAYERS

Thank you for reading this book, I pray that it has blessed you. In this chapter, I put together prayers I feel will help you grow as a believer. Pray these prayers, memorize them and meditate over them. They have helped me, my family and my church.

PRAYERS OF REPENTANCE

1. We / I REPENT of all unrighteousness and behavior that results in drawing from the wells of unrighteousness, wells of doubt and unbelief, wells of sin and selfishness.

2. We / I REPENT of wickedness and debauchery from the wells of unrighteousness; that results in idolatry and pride and self-rule.

3. We dig wells of humility and obedience to Your voice.

4. We dig wells of righteousness and holiness.

5. We dig wells of meekness and peace in this place.

6. We / I REPENT of all kinds of sexual perversion, of incest, of adultery and infidelity, of fornication and lasciviousness, and all uncleanness from these wells. We call an end to the reign of these things in our lives.

7. We / I REPENT for participating in these activities, whether for ourselves, or on behalf of others in this city and in this country.

8. We call an end to injustice in this city and this Nation.

9. We / I REPENT of injustice that has clogged the wells of righteousness in this city.

10. We / I REPENT of bigotry and hatred in OUR City and OUR Nation. Remove positions and postures, attitudes and language of racism, of prejudice and snobbery that are in our communities, and ministries.

11. We / I REPENT of thievery, of stealing, of cheating, of defrauding and dishonesty.

12. We call for honesty and integrity to be established: wells of honesty to be dug, wells of integrity to be dug, wells of holiness to be dug.

13. We / I REPENT of dishonoring our parents, dishonoring spiritual Fathers, and despising authorities that have been ordained by God.

14. We / I REPENT of speaking bad of, and being critical of, people and ministries and leaders in my City and Nation.

15. We / I REPENT of rebellion and anarchy in our lives and in this place.

16. We remove the debris of unrighteous rule from this place.

17. We remove the debris of unrighteous government from this place.

18. The debris of the unholy ambitions of men we remove from these wells in this place.

19. We call holiness to come, righteousness to come, justice to come, restitution to come, restoration to come to this place.

20. Forgive us, Lord, for our failings and for our silence before You concerning these things. We call on Your mercy Lord, to deliver us and heal us, in Jesus' name.

THANKSGIVING

1. Thank You Father, that You are drawing men and women, boys and girls to this city for this time; people who hear Your voice fresh and clear, people who can see what You want to do in this place; people with a fresh perspective; people that have not succumbed to the disbelief and unbelief of many in the city.

2. Thank You that gathering believers in this city is the fulfillment of Your prophetic purposes; purposes for which You have established times and seasons. Thank You that You are gathering those who once had come to this city, but were scattered away. Thank You that they will come with fresh eyes, with fresh ears, and with fresh voices.

3. Thank You that they will speak and declare fresh things. They will sing new songs. They will dream new dreams and hope for new things for this city.

4. Thank You, Father, that it is time for this city to come forth and for those in their caves to come out.

5. Thank You that for this city and this Nation, it is a new day. The old has been decommissioned and no longer can remain. Thank You that it is time for a new method and move in this city.
   - I call it to come.
   - I call it to come quickly and without delay.
   - I call Your servants in to find their places.
   - I call them to come running.
   - I call them to come together and cry out "DELIVERANCE COME"—It is your assignment to come. This day shall you arrive. This day shall you find your fulfillment in this city. This day is here!"

PART FOUR — EFFECTUAL FERVENT PRAYERS

- We declare, decree, and proclaim "DELIVERANCE COME".

6. Thank You for Your mercy to help us to embrace what You are doing in this time.

7. Thank You for granting us the courage to follow Your voice.

8. Thank You that in this place, as men and women we desire to know and hear the voice of God.

9. Thank You that You will silence the voices of those who offer no hope.

10. Thank You for raising up the apostolic and prophetic voices in this city and in this county and in this region to speak to the heavens and the earth and usher in the move of God for this time.

11. Thank You for raising up men and women to speak deliverance to this city; that You are raising up men and women who will say "Yes" to You and Your purposes.

12. Thank You that You are raising up children to speak life to this city, to be able to go forth and bring healing as You guide their lives in this day.

13. Thank You that the youth of this city will not be lost, but will find their Deliverer and their purpose in the things of God in this time.

14. Thank You that they will be given a place to obey Your voice freely.

15. Thank You that the rivers of the young, the rivers of the old, the

rivers of the rich, and the rivers of the poor will be able to flow in the things of God in this city. Their voice shall be heard loud and long.
- They shall speak deliverance and deliverance shall come.
- They shall speak wholeness and wholeness shall come.
- They shall speak life and life shall come.
- They shall speak to dead bones and dead bones shall live again!
- They shall speak and You will hear, Lord.
- Thank You for doing so, even now Lord, in Jesus' name.

16. Lord, We rejoice that we will see You moving in this city. That it will swell larger and larger, greater and greater. It will wash and cleanse, refresh and restore.

17. Thank You that this move will have strength and will accomplish all You desire for it.

18. Thank You that this will be a move that will bless the people and bless the nations.

19. Thank You, Father that this day is here. This day—it has begun!

20. Thank You, Father that You have Baptist rivers, Methodist rivers, Presbyterian rivers, Catholic rivers, Pentecostal rivers, Charismatic rivers, and all kinds of rivers.

21. Thank You that the water of Your Spirit will flow long and deep from these rivers.

22. Thank You, Father, that You watch over Your Word to perform it.

23. Thank You for making us rivers in Your Kingdom; that You teach us how to flow in the Spirit.

24. Thank You that as we create the rivers of revival, that rivers of renewal and rivers of restoration begin to flow (Eze.42).

25. Thank You that the water of Your spirit is beginning to flow more and more, minute by minute, hour by hour, day by day, week by week, month by month, year by year.

26. Thank You, Father, for bringing the thirsty to the rivers and that the rivers will be ready to provide.

27. Thank You, Father, that the rivers of salvation are flowing in this time; the rivers of healing, the rivers of deliverance, the rivers of the manifestations of Your Spirit all are being released in this time.

28. Thank You that rivers of prosperity and blessing flow in this time.

29. Thank You that poverty and wickedness that have flowed in this place cease their flow. Wells of wickedness dry up.

30. Thank You that rivers of provision, and invention, rivers of ingenuity, rivers of Godly ideas flow in this place.

31. Thank You, Father, that the favor of God flows in this city like a mighty river.

32. Thank You, Father, that wells of prophetic intercession are being dug.
    - Wells of worship are being dug.
    - Wells of insight and revelation are being dug.
    - Wells of truth and wisdom are being dug in this time.

33. Thank You that the Spirit of Truth reigns in this place.

34. Decree: Falsehood shall give way to Truth; the false shall give way to the True.

35. Thank You that deception and manipulation shall cease.

36. The strivings of men shall cease.

37. The ambitions of men shall cease and be replaced by obedience to Your plans and purposes.

38. Lord, Your purposes shall prevail. Your plans shall succeed. Your dreams shall see their day of fulfillment in this city. Those that prayed that this place would be a place of blessing for many shall see their prayers fulfilled.

39. Thank You that You teach us to dig our wells large enough for the tasks at hand.

40. Thank You that You show us how to dig these wells properly, Lord.

41. Thank You for Your mercy toward us, Lord, in Jesus' name.

42. Father, we dig wells of worship in this time. We call worshippers to come to this place.

43. We call intercessors to come, we call pray-ers to come. We call the apostles, the prophets, the evangelists, the pastors and the teachers to come to this place for this time. We call the minstrels and psalmists to come to this place for this time.

44. We call an end to strife and exclusionism that exists in the church.

45. We call for a return to our first love to come into the churches in this place.

46. We pray for righteous men and women to find their places of leadership in the churches and ministries of this city.

PROCLAMATIONS, DECREES AND DECLARATIONS

1. Father, we DECREE the release of the gathering angels to go forth and gather everything that pertains to the kingdom of God. Go forth, gather the finances, gather the key contacts, and gather the harvest of souls. Father, we speak that there is a gathering together of the angels and they are moving now to fulfill everything that you have ordained for this day, this week, this month, and this year.

2. We / I DECREE that there is a divine preparation of the harvest of finances.

3. We / I DECREE that there is divine preparation of the harvest of souls.

4. We / I DECREE that there is a divine preparation of the harvest of laborers to go into the vineyard and reap the harvest that is ripe and ready.

5. We / I DECREE that God's kingdom army will go forth and that there is now a receiving of all things that are now released by God but have not yet been manifest.

6. We / I DECREE that everything comes into proper position and alignment, and then be released pertaining to the end time wealth transfers into the hands of God's people.

7. We / I DECLARE the plans and purposes of God to be established in this place. We call these purposes to go forth and take their place in the earth.

8. We / I DECREE that the metroplex /our/my region will come

PART FOUR — EFFECTUAL FERVENT PRAYERS

under the authority and control of the kingdom of God; that there will be unity among key ministries, apostles and prophets, evangelists and pastors.

9. We / I DECREE that major strategies will be enacted in the region, that promote the Kingdom of God and establish exactly what God's plan is for the metroplex/ our/my region.

10. We / I DECREE that the funding for those God ordered projects of God's people would be located and released into their hands.

11. We / I DECREE that our/my children would now take up their rightful position in the Kingdom of God and in the ministry of the gospel of Jesus Christ. That the glory of God is so manifest in our/my lives that our physical bodies line up in health to the victory and glory manifest in our spiritual bodies. And we thank you for the full manifestation of these things in Jesus Mighty name.

12. Lord because we / I do not fear, we PROCLAIM that you empower us to walk and receive all the abundance of the Kingdom.

13. We / I PROCLAIM Your rule and dominion.

14. We / I PROCLAIM Your reign.

15. We / I PROCLAIM Your royalty.

16. We / I PROCLAIM Your riches.

17. We / I PROCLAIM Your righteousness.

18. We / I PROCLAIM and embrace the full dimension of Your Kingdom in our/my lives. Father it is Your delight and it brings

You great satisfaction to give us/me the dominion rule of the King through our lives.

19. We / I PROCLAIM and decree the Kingdom of God and His dominion, in our lives, in our churches, in this region, in all areas of finance, and over this nation.

20. We / I PROCLAIM the Kingdom of God is expanding into the areas that were strongholds of the enemy, into the school systems, into the economic systems, into the political system, into the social and media systems and into every area that You have ordained in this season.

21. We / I PROCLAIM and DECREE the Kingdom of God's impact upon the lives of men and women who don't know the glorious benefits of your kingdom, and that these benefits are being manifested now.

22. We / I PROCLAIM and DECREE the Kingdom of God's success in everything that you have purposed and planned to be accomplished in this land and in the earth.

23. We / I DECLARE we cannot be destroyed by the weapons of the enemy because of the righteousness of the Kingdom of God.

24. We / I DECREE and DECLARE Satan's weapons are nullified against us, and all that we represent here.

25. We / I DECLARE and claim Your peace, Your righteousness, Your security and Your triumph over demonic opposition.

26. We / I DECLARE rule, reign with royalty, righteousness and riches into every aspect of our lives, and into our entire existence.

PART FOUR — EFFECTUAL FERVENT PRAYERS

27. We / I PROCLAIM and DECLARE that Your will is being established and done in every aspect of our existence, because the Kingdom is in place.

28. We / I PROCLAIM and DECLARE that the Kingdom will rule in us as we execute God's instructions that He has revealed to us.

29. We / I PROCLAIM and DECLARE that the Kingdom will reign in the earthly realm (all earthy matters concerning us) according to God's will.

30. We / I PROCLAIM and DECLARE that Kingdom riches will be manifested in and produced through the lives of His sons and daughters in the earth.

31. We / I PROCLAIM and DECLARE that Kingdom royalty would be expressed and exhibited in every aspect of our lives (that we may walk as God's royal priesthood in the earth).

32. We / I PROCLAIM and DECLARE that the righteousness of God is breaking forth in the earth through the lives of His Kingdom sons and daughters.

33. We / I DECLARE the Kingdom has come in your people and your will is being done in the earth through declaring the Gospel of the Kingdom.

34. We / I PROCLAIM that the Holy Spirit has gone forth in agreement with the design of Your will to establish the Kingdom of God in the earth.

35. We / I DECREE that the Holy Spirit will work out the will of God in our finances and in world affairs that pertain to the Kingdom of God.

36. We / I DECREE that God's will of salvation is coming to our families and to the families of the earth.

37. We / I PROCLAIM that the Spirit of the living God is working out the will of God in every area of need in our lives.

38. We / I PROCLAIM and DECLARE the will of God to be accomplished today, this week and over all of our affairs.

39. We / I PROCLAIM and DECLARE that today our daily bread is provided, and that everything we need for our lives is given to us "according to His riches in glory by Christ Jesus."

40. We / I PROCLAIM and DECLARE that "the order of heaven" is being accomplished in the earth by the Holy Ghost.

41. Spirit of the living God, bring into full manifestation God's will in the lives of the people. Bring into full manifestation God's will in every city and nation. Let the Kingdom of God come and the will of God be accomplished, in the exact order and function that it is being accomplished in heaven today.

42. We / I DECREE and DECLARE that in the same way that there is a manifestation of victory over the powers of darkness in heaven, this day we declare that there is a manifestation of victory over the powers of darkness in the earth.

43. We / I PROCLAIM and DECREE that in the same way there is divine provision and abundance in heaven, this day we declare that there is divine provision and abundance in His people and in our lives here on the earth.

44. We / I DECLARE Jesus Christ openly before men, and that Jesus has given us the keys to the Kingdom of heaven. So we

PART FOUR — EFFECTUAL FERVENT PRAYERS

DECLARE unlawful this day, everything that seeks to hinder, block or frustrate Your people from declaring You openly and exercising their kingdom authority in the earth. Father we thank You that You're downloading, by the Holy Spirit, specific instructions to Your people in every situation.

45. We / I DECLARE Jesus as Messiah and Lord and we thank You Holy Ghost that we receive the knowledge that we need for every moment of our existence in this world. We PROCLAIM the Spirit of God, be released now to go forth and carry out God's will in the earth, in this nation, in this region, in this city, in this community and in our lives. Jesus we thank You that heaven will back what we declare in the earth through the Kingdom of God by the Holy Spirit. So we operate our authority in this prayer according to what heaven has ordained.

46. We / I DECREE that this is the day that the Lord has made, and we walk in all the benefits, the anointing, the revelation and the prosperity that God has designed for our lives.

47. We / I DECREE and DECLARE that the anointing that breaks yokes and bondage is released here and now.

48. We / I DECREE unusual miracles and gifts of healing all over this place.

49. We / I DECREE signs and wonders are manifesting all around me.

50. We / I DECREE an out-pouring of God's Spirit in this place, in my church and in my ministry.

51. We / I DECREE that angels are engaging in warfare on our behalf, and that demonic powers are being subdued.

52. Father, we thank you that you have entrusted the mysteries of the Kingdom of God to us, even your secret counsel that you have hidden from the ungodly.

53. We / I DECLARE this day that we are led by the Spirit of God and that we are the sons of God in the earth. This day through our obedience to the Holy Spirit, we reverse the effects of the curse that has come upon our nation, our city, and our families. We reverse the effects of the curse that has affected our nation, our city, and our families.

54. We / I DECLARE that the sons of God are manifest in the earth and have the answer to the world's problems. Through our Kingdom authority, we DECLARE that our nation, our churches, our families and our individual lives are totally restored to what God ordained them to be before Adam's disobedience. Father, we claim the fully restored rights over our family, our finances and our destiny.

PART FOUR — EFFECTUAL FERVENT PRAYERS

DECLARE, DECREE, PROCLAIM

We commission Apostolic declarations *"To proclaim the acceptable year of the LORD, and the day of vengeance of our God; to comfort all who mourn"* (Isaiah 61:2).

1. We declare, decree, and proclaim the acceptable year of the Lord, the year of the Lord's favor, and Jubilee.

2. We decree, declare and proclaim that He is anointing us to carry out this mandate.

3. We make a decree *"Hear 0 heavens and earth...let heaven and earth give witness!"* *"Give ear, 0 heavens, and I will speak; and hear 0 earth, the words of my mouth"* (Deuteronomy 32:1). *"Hear 0 heavens, and give ear, 0 earth! For the LORD has spoken.."* (Isaiah 1:2)

JUBILEE AND FAVOR

1. We decree and declare Jubilee—that total deliverance for us has come, cancellation of debts for each of us and our families, and liberation from any kind of a bondage, taskmaster, or oppression over our lives. In this anointing, we can proclaim "Jubilee!" and set into motion, the power and the force that causes everything in our lives to begin to come into divine order. In the year of Jubilee God's word declares, the angels of heaven act upon that decree, and a supernatural endowment of power comes into our lives that we never had before.

2. We decree the Spirit of the Lord God is upon us to proclaim "Favor!" Everything around us will begin to change because of the favor of God.

3. One moment this power will be released under the anointing, and we proclaim, "Favor, favor, favor!" We declare favor has come suddenly.

4. We declare a release of the spirit of grace upon us, through the blood of JESUS and a supernatural endowment of power.

5. We declare that in this Jubilee our day of vindication is coming, to *"proclaim the acceptable year of the LORD, and the day of vengeance of our God; to comfort all who mourn"* (Isaiah 61:2).

6. Now we declare and decree the day of the vengeance of our God. He is releasing an anointing upon us so that we can call court into session and call heaven to be our witness, when there is injustice. In this anointing to declare God's vindication *(Definition— vindication: defending against criticism or censure [Webster's Dictionary])*, we can access the heavenly court system where the

Holy Ghost presides as our advocate and counselor in matters concerning our lives, destiny, inheritance, and death.

7. We declare that sickness, disease, death, poverty, bondage, oppression and false accusations are illegal, and that there is a reversal NOW.

8. We decree that all kinds of injustice, is being turned NOW by the Spirit of the Lord that is upon us to declare vindication. We know the scripture where God says, *"Vengeance is Mine, I will repay,' says the Lord"* (Hebrews 10:30), but He has invited us, as saints of God, into a place of the power of the decree.

9. We decree God's word prevails and disarms injustice in the heavenly realm for divine judgment against our enemies.

INTERCESSION

1. Lord, establish the rivers of healing in this city, the rivers of deliverance in this city, the rivers of salvation, the rivers of spiritual maturity in this city, the rivers of love and peace in this city, and the rivers of worship in this city (Psalm 1:3).

2. Lord, restore the rivers of Godly commerce here, the rivers of invention, the rivers of Godly education here, and the rivers of music and art in this city.

3. Lord, we call rivers of healing, rivers of intercession, rivers of provision, rivers of salvation and deliverance to be established here. We call rivers of understanding and divine order; rivers of interpretation of Your plans and purposes to be established here.

4. We declare the plans and purposes of God to be established in this place. We call these purposes to go forth and take their place in the earth.

5. Lord, we call for an open heaven in this place. A place where men and women, boys and girls can hear Your voice strong and clear; where men and women, boys and girls hear and obey all Your instructions.

PART FOUR — EFFECTUAL FERVENT PRAYERS

APOSTOLIC DECREES OF JUSTICE AND PEACE

Apostolic Decrees of Justice outline God's mandate for this season.

1. We / I declare The Spirit of revelation, which illuminates the power of decrees, declarations and proclamations in the Court of the heavens.

2. By decree and proclamation we / I release the anointing of Jesus the intercessor, to declare favor in the heavenly courts, and release the activity of blessing in God's throne room, to give me / you / us an expected end, according to God's will here on Earth.

3. We / I commission Apostolic and Prophetic declarations, that are in heaven and sent by God, to have tremendous authority to bring about His justice and peace in our Nation, our Cities, our ministries, our families and our lives.

4. We / I decree that the Lord will release significant breakthroughs when we proclaim His will and His word.

PRAYER & DECLARATION FOR THE SPIRITUAL LEADERS OF THE CITY

1. We proclaim, declare and decree success, blessing and favor for the apostles and prophets, the evangelists, the pastors and teachers, those that lead churches in this city.

2. We proclaim, declare and decree that the Spirit of wisdom and revelation in the knowledge of You be unveiled in their lives this day.

3. We proclaim, declare and decree that You would grant them a comprehension of what is the anointing you have given them to fulfill their mandate for the Kingdom of God—that the anointing of God would increase upon their lives.

4. We proclaim, declare and decree that they have the anointing, grace and heart of compassion for the people they shepherd and for this nation and city.

5. We proclaim, declare and decree they have peace in their homes, marriages and their families.

6. We proclaim, declare and decree a hedge of protection about them and about their families and their possessions.

7. We proclaim, declare and decree that righteousness is working in them.

8. We proclaim, declare and decree clear understanding of their purpose in this time in this city.

9. We bind strife, envy, and the spirit of division and trouble of any

PART FOUR — EFFECTUAL FERVENT PRAYERS

sort. We revoke their right to operate in this city, in the churches of this city, or in the leadership of the churches.

10. We proclaim, declare and decree UNITY amongst the brethren, unity in the churches, and unity in the Body of Christ.

11. We proclaim, declare and decree the kingdom of God to come into this city, into the leadership of the churches in this city and into the congregations in this city.

12. We proclaim, declare and decree a release of finances to the churches and ministries of this city.

13. We bind the spirit of financial control that has operated in this city and declare to that spirit, that it is bound and its power broken over the finances of this city.

14. We proclaim, declare and decree financial breakthrough and freedom and deliverance from debt and financial burdens in this city.

15. We proclaim, declare and decree breakthrough and freedom and deliverance from the demonic spirits creating chaos through DRUGS, GANGS, SEXUAL PERVERSION, MURDERS and ABORTIONS.

16. We declare new levels of anointing, calling and appointments, released to shift the spiritual atmosphere and climate in this City; that the apostles, the prophets, the evangelists, the pastors and the teachers would arise in this city this day in Jesus' name.

17. We proclaim and decree a release of signs and wonders in this city, and declare that every gift of God that is in the people of God would be released now, in Jesus' name.

TEACH US TO PRAY

THE LORD'S PRAYER

Matthew 6:9–13 (KJV)

After this manner therefore pray ye: Our Father which art in heaven, Hallowed be thy name. Thy kingdom come. Thy will be done in earth, as it is in heaven. Give us this day our daily bread. And forgive us our debts, as we forgive our debtors. And lead us not into temptation, but deliver us from evil: For thine is the kingdom, and the power, and the glory, forever. Amen.

Psalm 23:1–6 (KJV)

The Lord is my shepherd; I shall not want. He maketh me to lie down in green pastures: he leadeth me beside the still waters. He restoreth my soul: he leadeth me in the paths of righteousness for his name's sake. Yea, though I walk through the valley of the shadow of death, I will fear no evil: for thou art with me; thy rod and thy staff they comfort me. Thou preparest a table before me in the presence of mine enemies: thou anointest my head with oil; my cup runneth over. Surely goodness and mercy shall follow me all the days of my life: and I will dwell in the house of the Lord forever.

PART FOUR — EFFECTUAL FERVENT PRAYERS

PRAYERS FROM PSALM 91 (Psalm 91:1–16 KJV)

1. He that dwells in the secret place of the Most High shall abide under the shadow of the Almighty.

2. I will say of the Lord , He is my refuge and my fortress: my God; in him will I trust.

3. Surely he shall deliver thee from the snare of the fowler, and from the noisome pestilence.

4. He shall cover thee with his feathers, and under his wings shalt thou trust: his truth shall be thy shield and buckler.

5. Thou shalt not be afraid for the terror by night; nor for the arrow that flieth by day;

6. Nor for the pestilence that walketh in darkness; nor for the destruction that wasteth at noonday.

7. A thousand shall fall at thy side, and ten thousand at thy right hand; but it shall not come nigh thee.

8. Only with thine eyes shalt thou behold and see the reward of the wicked.

9. Because thou hast made the Lord , which is my refuge, even the most High, thy habitation;

10. There shall no evil befall thee, neither shall any plague come nigh thy dwelling.

TEACH US TO PRAY

INDEX

PART ONE
Introduction
[1] Wikipedia
[2] 2 Corinthians 10:4–6
[3] John 16:13

Different Strokes for Different Types
[1] Hosea 4:6
[2] Luke 11:1
[3] James 5:6
[4] Proverbs 25:2

Thanksgiving Prayer
[1] Football team based in England
[2] 1 Thessalonians 5:16–18
[3] John 10:10
[4] James 4:7
[5] Romans 1:21–31
[6] Luke 17:12–18

Praise & Worship Prayer
[1] Psalms 48:1
[2] Great Connection by Bonnie Deuschle
[3] Isaiah 43:21
[4] Mark 4:41

Intercession
[1] 1 John 3:11
[2] 1 John 3:16
[3] Colossians 1:3
[4] Philippians 1:4
[5] Ephesians 1:16
[6] 2 Thessalonians 1:11

Travail
[1] Daniel 2
[2] Daniel 6:18
[3] 2 Corinthians 5:17
[4] Isaiah 42:9
[5] Isaiah 48:3–7
[6] Galatians 4:19

Groaning
[1] John 11:14
[2] John 11:19
[3] John 11:33
[4] John 11:38
[5] John 11:43
[6] Psalms 102:5
[7] Romans 8:22–23
[8] Psalms 42:7

Supplication and Petition
[1] Matthew 7:7
[2] Proverbs 18:23
[3] Hebrews 7:7
[4] 2 Chronicles 14:4
[5] 2 Chronicles 14:6
[6] 2 Chronicles 14:11
[7] 2 Chronicles 14:13
[8] 2 Chronicles 16:7–8
[9] 2 Chronicles 16:12
[10] Mark 10:46–52
[11] Philippians 4:6

Blessing Prayer
[1] Numbers 23:7
[2] Numbers 23:20–21
[3] Luke 3:22

Confessions of Sins
[1] Acts 13:22 (Author's emphasis)
[2] Psalms 51:1–12
[3] Psalms 24:2–3
[4] 1 Peter 1:16

Confession of the Word
[1] Proverbs 18:21
[2] James 3:3–6
[3] Psalms 119:13
[4] Isaiah 55:11

Declarations
[1] 2 Peter 1:25
[2] Romans 4:17
[3] Genesis 1:3
[4] Mark 11:23
[5] John 10:34–35
[6] Genesis 1:28
[7] Proverbs 30:29–31

Decrees
[1] Esther 3:9–12 (Author's emphasis)
[2] Esther 8:3–5 (Author's emphasis)
[3] Esther 8:8 (Author's emphasis)
[4] Daniel 6:14
[5] Daniel 6:14
[6] Daniel 6:15
[7] Genesis 3:17–19
[8] Genesis 3:16
[9] Joshua 24:15
[10] 1 Kings 8:25
[11] Matthew 19:28

Directed Prevailing Prayers
[1] 2 Corinthians 1:20
[2] Luke 11:11–13 (Author's emphasis)
[3] 1 Kings 18:42–45
[4] Luke 2:25–38
[5] Hebrews 6:12
[6] Hebrews 10:35–39 (Author's emphasis)

INDEX

Shouting & Yelling Prayer
[1] 1 Samuel 3:1
[2] 1 Samuel 4:5–7
[3] Joshua 6:1
[4] Wikipedia
[5] Joshua 6:20

Metaphoric Prayer
[1] Exodus 17:8–13

Demonstration & Dedication Prayers
[1] Romans 1:25

Sacks and Ashes
[1] Nehemiah 9:1
[2] Isaiah 57:15
[3] Matthew 6:16–18

Praying in the Spirit
[1] John 7:38
[2] Ezekiel 47:8–12
[3] 1 Thessalonians 5:17

Concert Prayers
[1] Leviticus 26:8
[2] Matthew 18:16
[3] Mark 14:33 (Author's emphasis)
[4] Romans 15:30
[5] Maximized Manhood—Ed Cole
[6] Communication, Sex and Money—Ed Cole

Spiritual Warfare Prayers
[1] Daniel 10:12–13
[2] 1 Thessalonians 2:18

Meditation Prayer
[1] Psalms 19:14
[2] Joshua 1:8
[3] 1 Thessalonians 5:17
[4] Luke 10:40–42 (Author's emphasis)

Weeping Prayer
[1] John 2:35
[2] 2 Corinthians 12:9
[3] James 4:8

Apostolic Rank Prayers
[1] Luke 12:48
[2] Mark 4:8
[3] Matthew 25:15
[4] 1 Chronicles 12:38
[5] Joel 2:7
[6] James 5:14
[7] 1 Timothy 4:14

Prophetic Prayer
[1] 1 Corinthians 14:3
[2] 1 Corinthians 14:4
[3] Numbers 11:29
[4] Amos 3:7
[5] 2 Peter 1:21 (Author's emphasis)
[6] 1 John 4:1

<u>Sacrificial Prayer</u>
[1] Acts 10:2
[2] Acts 10:4
[3] 1 Kings 3:5
[4] Revelations 11:15

PART TWO
<u>Why Pray?</u>
[1] 2 Peter 1:12–15
[2] James 4:3
[3] Matthew 6:7

PART THREE
<u>Heavenly Court System</u>
[1] Il Cenacolo or L 'Ultima Cena— 15th century mural painted in Milan
[2] Matthew 17:1–5
[3] Matthew 19:28
[4] 1 Corinthians 3:6
[5] Mark 10:35–40
[6] Isaiah 6:5
[7] Revelation 1:17
[8] Daniel 7:9–10
[9] 1 Kings 22:19–23
[10] Deuteronomy 9:28
[11] Acts 15:28 (Author's emphasis)
[12] Hebrews 2:6–7

INDEX

TEACH US TO PRAY

Printed in Dunstable, United Kingdom